PUNJABI DIASPORA AND THEIR CREATIVE EFFORTS FOR NATION-BUILDING

About the Author

Dr. Neelu Rawat is an Associate Professor and Head of the Department of Sociology at the Central University of Punjab, Bathinda, India. With a specialization in Sociology of Change and Development, Tribal Studies, Women's Studies, and Diaspora Studies, she has established herself as a leading academician and researcher in the field of social sciences. She holds an M.A. and Ph.D. in Sociology and has qualified NET and SET, along with being a recipient of Prestige's fellowships. Over the course of her career, Dr. Rawat has made extensive contributions through teaching, research, and academic leadership. She has supervised Ph.D. scholars and guided dissertations at the postgraduate level.

Dr. Rawat has a prolific research record, with good number of publications in UGC CARE listed, SCOPUS, and peer-reviewed journals, along with book chapters, commentaries, and a forthcoming manuscript. She has also presented a number of papers in national and international seminars and conferences, delivered invited lectures, and contributed MOOC lectures, e-content, and course materials for national platforms like SWAYAM and IGNOU.

PUNJABI DIASPORA AND THEIR CREATIVE EFFORTS FOR NATION-BUILDING

A Socio-Cultural and Historical Perspective

Neelu Rawat

CONCEPT PUBLISHING COMPANY PVT. LTD.
NEW DELHI - 110 059

ISBN: 978-93-6344-309-9

First Published 2026

Published and Printed by

Since1974

Concept Publishing Company Pvt. Ltd.
A/15-16, Commercial Block, Mohan Garden
New Delhi-110059 (India)
T: +91-11-41101460
E: publishing@conceptpub.com, *W*: www.conceptpub.com

Cataloging in Publication--Courtesy: D.K. Agencies (P) Ltd. <docinfo@dkagencies.com>

Rawat, Neelu, author.

Punjabi diaspora and their creative efforts for nation-building : a socio-cultural and historical perspective / Neelu Rawat.

pages cm

Includes bibliographical references and index.

ISBN 9789363443099

1. Sikh diaspora. 2. Panjabis (South Asian people)--India--Bhatinda--Migrations. 3. Panjabis (South Asian people)--India--Barnala (District)--Migrations. 4. Panjabis (South Asian people)--India--Jalandhar (Punjab)--Migrations. 5. Panjabis (South Asian people)--Foreign countries--Intellectual life. 6. Punjab (India)--Emigration and immigration--Social aspects. 7. Punjab (India)--Emigration and immigration--Economic aspects. 8. Punjab (India)--Emigration and immigration--Political aspects. I. Title.

LCC DS432.S5R39 2026 | DDC 304.80954552 23

Central University of Punjab, Bathinda
Established vide an Act no. 25(2009) of Parliament

Prof. Raghavendra P. Tiwari
Vice Chancellor

Ref No. CUPB/VCO/2025/FWD

Dated: 9th December 2025

Foreword

The study of diaspora has long occupied a central place in understanding the intersections of migration, identity, and globalization. In an increasingly interconnected world, diasporic communities have emerged not only as agents of cultural transmission but also as significant contributors to social, political, and economic transformations across nations. Within this larger context, the book titled *Punjabi Diaspora and Their Creative Efforts for Nation-Building* authored by Dr Neelu Rawat, stand out as a timely and valuable contribution to sociological discourse. It deepens our comprehension of how transnational communities, especially the Punjabi diaspora, shape, sustain, and reinterpret connections between the homeland and host societies. By situating the discussion within broader theoretical frameworks of migration, transnationalism, and cultural hybridity, the author successfully bridges historical legacies with contemporary realities. The narrative traverses the early colonial phase of indentured labour and overseas settlement, the post-Independence wave of skilled migration, and the globalization driven mobility of recent decades. In doing so, the book contextualizes the Punjabi experience within the larger Indian diasporic fabric, showing how historical trajectories and cultural memories continue to shape present-day identities.

One of the book's notable strengths lies in its ability to blend sociological theory with rich empirical evidence. The study does not merely chronicle the economic or demographic dimensions of migration; rather, it delves deeply into the lived experiences of the diaspora as they negotiate belonging, sustain kinship ties, and create hybrid cultural spaces that embody both tradition and modernity. Through this lens, the book highlights the dynamic interplay between continuity and change, showing how diasporic Punjabis retain their linguistic and cultural roots while simultaneously adapting to diverse socio-political environments abroad. Equally commendable is the author's nuanced engagement with the challenges faced by the diaspora. The book addresses generational identity shifts, the pressures of assimilation, and the often complex emotional negotiations of belonging and alienation that mark the migrant experience. It raises critical questions about how second and third-generation Punjabis relate to their ancestral homeland and how cultural continuity is maintained in the face of global modernity. These discussions extend the scope of the book beyond celebration, inviting a balanced understanding of diaspora as a site of both empowerment and contestation.

The exploration of the Punjabi diaspora's role in **Nation-Building** adds a distinctive dimension to the work. The book insightfully documents the community's philanthropic contributions to education, health care, and rural development, as well as their engagement in cultural diplomacy and social reform. By examining their creative expressions in literature, music, cinema, and digital media, the author illuminates how the diaspora continues to shape narratives of identity and belonging.

The emphasis on "glocal" linkages, where global experiences are reinterpreted through local cultural idioms, underscores the significance of diasporic agency in shaping not only community life abroad but also the sociocultural landscape of Punjab itself. What makes this volume particularly engaging is its humanistic spirit. Beyond its academic merit, the book resonates with empathy, respect, and recognition for the migrants whose journeys form its core narrative. It celebrates their creativity, resilience, and enduring connection to their roots, even as it acknowledges the struggles and sacrifices that underpin their success stories. In tracing the evolution of diasporic identities, the author reminds us that migration is not merely a movement across space but a profound reconfiguration of selfhood, belonging and cultural continuity. For scholars and students of sociology, cultural studies, and history, this book offers an invaluable resource that combines theoretical sophistication with empirical richness. For policymakers and practitioners, it provides insights into diaspora engagement, migration governance, and cultural preservation. And for general readers, it presents a compelling narrative that captures the human dimensions of mobility, identity, and globalization.

Ultimately, the book *Punjabi Diaspora and Their Creative Efforts for Nation-Building* exemplify scholarship that is both intellectually rigorous and socially meaningful. It bridges the worlds of academia and lived experience, of historical memory and contemporary relevance. The author's commitment to understanding diaspora not merely as a demographic phenomenon but as a deeply human, creative, and **Nation-Building** force is both admirable and inspiring. I am confident that this book will stimulate fresh dialogue and research in diaspora studies and serve as a foundation for further inquiry into how migrant communities continue to redefine notions of culture, identity, and belonging in a globalized era. It stands as a testament to the enduring spirit of the Punjabi diaspora and to the power of scholarly inquiry in illuminating the ever-evolving relationship between people, place, and **Nation-Building**.

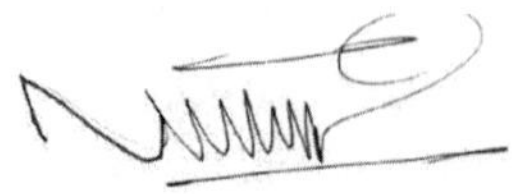

(Raghavendra P. Tiwari)
Vice-Chancellor

Central University of Punjab, VPO-Ghudda, Bathinda, Punjab, India-151401

Preface

The story of migration is, in many ways, the story of humanity itself. From the earliest journeys of nomadic groups to the vast movements driven by trade, conquest, colonization, and globalization, the act of crossing borders has been central to the shaping of civilizations. Migration has not only reshaped geographies but has also redefined identities, created hybrid cultures, and forged enduring bonds that transcend political and territorial boundaries. It is through the lens of migration that we can best understand the interplay of continuity and change in human societies.

Among the many diasporic experiences, the Indian diaspora occupies a unique and significant place in the global imagination. Today, with over thirty-two million people dispersed across North America, Europe, Africa, the Middle East, Southeast Asia, and beyond, the Indian diaspora represents one of the largest, most dynamic, and culturally influential transnational communities in the world. The diaspora offers a rich sociological and historical canvas to study pressing questions of belonging, hybridity, integration, identity politics, and transnational linkages.

This book seeks to situate the Indian diaspora within its layered historical, social, and cultural contexts, while examining the complex ways in which Indian communities abroad have negotiated their identities amidst shifting global orders. The Indian diaspora's story is not linear but textured stretching from the colonial past, when indentured labourers were transported across the seas under exploitative contracts, to the post-independence era, which witnessed the rise of a highly mobile and globally connected professional class. Each wave of migration carried with it stories of resilience, struggle, aspiration, and transformation.

In engaging with their host societies, diasporic Indians have contributed in diverse ways: through cultural expressions that blend tradition and innovation; entrepreneurial ventures that strengthen economies; political and civic participation that shapes governance; and philanthropic engagements that sustain developmental initiatives in both their host countries and the homeland. The diaspora, therefore, is not merely a community in exile or dispersal, but an active agent of globalization, bridging worlds and creating new forms of connectedness.

Within this larger framework, this book places particular emphasis on the Punjabi diaspora arguably one of the most vibrant, visible, and historically significant segments of the global Indian community. Punjabi migration has been shaped by multiple forces: colonial-era recruitment into the British Army and agrarian labour systems; the trauma and displacement following the Partition of 1947; and post-independence migration linked to economic pursuits, particularly in agriculture, industry, and small-scale enterprises. Punjabis have settled in large numbers in countries as diverse as Canada, the United States, the United Kingdom, Australia, and Malaysia, leaving an indelible imprint on these societies.

The Punjabi diaspora is not only known for its cultural vitality through music, cinema, literature, and religious traditions but also for its entrepreneurial spirit, political activism, and global networks. At the same time, it has remained deeply invested in Punjab, contributing remittances, supporting social and religious institutions, and engaging with the political and cultural life of the region. The story of the Punjabi diaspora thus embodies the tensions of displacement and belonging, tradition and modernity, rootedness and cosmopolitanism.

At its heart, this work is an exploration of how diasporic communities embody both fixity and fluidity. While anchored in traditions, they are also in constant negotiation with the demands of global modernity. Their journeys raise fundamental questions: How do diasporic communities preserve identity across generations? How do they navigate cultural hybridity? In what ways do they influence both their homelands and their host societies? And what lessons does their story hold for understanding the broader human condition in an era of unprecedented mobility and interconnectedness?

It is my hope that this book will serve not only as an academic contribution to the fields of migration studies, sociology, and cultural history but also as a reflection on the deeper meanings of movement, identity, and cultural continuity. By examining the experiences of the Indian and Punjabi diaspora, it seeks to illuminate the creative, resilient, and transformative spirit of communities that continue to shape the contours of an increasingly globalized world.

Bathinda **Neelu Rawat**

Acknowledgements

This book is the outcome of sustained intellectual engagement, collective support, and encouragement received from many individuals and institutions. I wish to express my deep sense of gratitude to all those who, in diverse ways, contributed to its completion.

First and foremost, I express my deepest gratitude to the Hon'ble Vice-Chancellor, Central University of Punjab, Bathinda, Prof. Raghavendra P. Tiwari for his visionary leadership, academic guidance, and constant encouragement have not only inspired this work but have also created an environment where scholarship thrives in the service of society.

I am profoundly thankful to Prof. S.N. Chaudhary and Prof. Pratima Chaudhary for their academic supervision and invaluable guidance throughout this journey.

My sincere gratitude extends to Dean in-Charge, Academics Prof. Ramakrishna Wusirika, and Director, Research and Development Cell, Prof. Anjana Munshi, Central University of Punjab, Bathinda, for fostering an academic environment and providing the encouragement necessary for pursuing this research. I also extend my sincere thanks to the library staff of the Central University of Punjab, whose support and resources greatly facilitated this research.

I am equally grateful to the respondents of the study, families, organizations, and other stakeholders for their constant support, insightful discussions, and constructive suggestions, all of which enriched this work. Special acknowledgment is due to the Punjabi diaspora communities across Canada, the United Kingdom, the United States, Australia, and the Middle East. Their narratives, creative expressions, and lived experiences have been a source of inspiration in conceptualizing this study, and their contributions to cultural preservation and Nation-building remain truly remarkable.

I owe immense gratitude to my students and research scholars, whose curiosity and probing questions continuously motivated me to explore new dimensions of migration, identity, cultural hybridity, and the broader processes of Nation-building. Their involvement has been invaluable in shaping the critical perspectives of this work.

On a personal note, I thank my family for their unwavering encouragement, patience, and emotional support throughout this academic journey. Their understanding made the process of writing this book both possible and meaningful.

Finally, I dedicate this book to the countless migrants who, in their journeys across borders, reconfigure cultures, identities, and communities. Their resilience, creativity, struggles, and contributions to Nation-building embody the very essence of diaspora, and it is to them that this work owes its deepest debt.

Neelu Rawat

Contents

1

Introduction

The Indian diaspora, a dynamic mosaic of mobility and cultural cross-pollination, represents the tension between fixity and fluidity. Transplanted and dispersed on the continents, the diaspora tread the tightrope of maintaining traditions transplanted and adapting to contemporary globalism, providing a particularly valuable lens with which to observe identity, place, and the Trans-figurative potential of global connections in today's interlinked world.

The Indian diaspora, with an estimated 32 million or more people worldwide, is a large and dispersed migrant community that has gained prominence as a research field in sociology. A highly dynamic and diverse population, Indian diaspora has settled in several parts of the world, such as North America, Europe, the Middle East, Southeast Asia, and Africa (Ministry of External Affairs, Government of India, 2023). From a sociological point of view, the Indian diaspora is an interesting case study of migration, identity construction, cultural hybridity, and transnationalism. This introduction systematically examines the historical, cultural, and social aspects of the Indian diaspora, emphasizing its contributions to world societies and challenges in preserving cultural continuity while accommodating host societies.

The Indian diaspora has its roots in historical processes such as colonialism, indentured labour, and post-colonial migration. During the 19th and early 20th centuries, the British Empire transported millions of Indians as indentured labourers to colonies in the Caribbean, Africa, and Southeast Asia to work on plantations (Tinker, 1974). This marked the first major wave of Indian migration, creating communities in countries like Trinidad and Tobago, Guyana, South Africa, and Fiji. Post-independence, a second wave of migration occurred, driven by economic opportunities and educational aspirations, particularly to Western countries such as the United States, Canada, and the United Kingdom (Vertovec, 2000). These migration patterns have shaped the socio-economic and cultural landscapes of both the host countries and India itself.

One of the key sociological themes in the study of the Indian diaspora is the negotiation of cultural identity. Diasporic communities often navigate a complex interplay between preserving their cultural heritage and assimilating into the host society. For instance, Indian Americans have successfully maintained cultural practices such as festivals (e.g., Diwali), cuisine, and language while also integrating into the multicultural fabric of the United States (Kurien, 2005). This process of cultural hybridity, where elements of Indian and host cultures merge, has led to the creation of unique diasporic identities. However, this hybridity is not without tension, as second and third-generation diaspora members often grapple with questions of belonging and authenticity (Bhatia & Ram, 2009).

This hybridity, as it is configured and understood using the framework of cultural sociology, is conditioned by constant negotiation, adaptation, and resistance in private and public domains. Identity in diaspora settings is neither an inherited fixed condition but rather a situated and performative construction conditioned by intergenerational conversation, racial and ethnic hierarchies, and host nation institutional structures. Borrowing from Stuart Hall's (1990) concept of identity as a "production", diasporic identity is constantly produced in relation to social and historical contingencies, and not based on a monolithic cultural essence. For the Indian diaspora, particularly in the case of second and third-generation migrants, identity formation is a dialectic process on the one side from family socialization emphasizing 'Indianness' in language, religion, and social norms, and on the other, engaging with wider societal cultures characterized by individualism, liberal values, and multicultural ethos. These identity negotiations are then further entangled by the racialized condition of being 'the other' in most Western societies, whereby diasporic subjects are subject to constant inclusion-exclusion navigation.

Cultural practices like maintaining Hindu or Sikh celebrations, learning regional languages like Tamil or Gujarati, or being part of diasporic religious institutions act as forms of cultural reproduction and symbolic boundary maintenance. Such practices reinforce group solidarity and shared memory but also undergo reinterpretation and, at times, challenge by younger generations in trying to harmonize inherited traditions with their lived experiences in diversely pluralized societies. For instance, Kurien (2007) documents that second-generation Indian Americans construct hybrid religious forms that synthesize devotional Hinduism with liberal spiritualities of values in their American environments. This hybridity is not merely additive but creative, producing novel forms of cultural life that challenge essentialist understandings of both Indian and Western identities. However, as Bhatia and Ram (2009) argue, these processes are often fraught with emotional ambivalence and social strain, particularly as younger members contend with pressures to conform to diasporic 'authenticity' while also experiencing marginality or alienation in the wider society.

Additionally, the institutional environment in which the diaspora is located schools, workplaces, immigration regulations, and media plays an important part in shaping identity trajectories. Schools, for example, become spaces in which diasporic youth meet cultural difference and negotiate their subjectivity in relation to hegemonic discourses regarding race, ethnicity, and national identity. Here, identity is a space of political contestation, where diasporic people challenge stereotypes and construct other narratives of self and community. The rise of diasporic advocacy groups, cultural organizations, and transnational networks demonstrate how identity is not only lived at the individual level but also collectively mobilized to seek recognition, rights, and representation. These movements complicate the conventional binaries of preservation and assimilation, proposing instead a continuum of practices across multiple geographies and cultural imaginaries (Appadurai, 1996; Vertovec, 2009).

Diasporic identity formation therefore arises not as a one-way process of adaptation to receiving culture, but as a dialogic negotiation between both the cultural practices of the place of origin and prevailing norms of receiving society. This dynamic becomes particularly apparent in intergenerational settings, in which younger diaspora individuals frequently resist both the traditionalist expectations of their elders and the racialized classification of dominant society (Hall, 1990; Bhatia & Ram, 2009). The "in-between" site which diasporic people occupy is one of ambivalence what Homi Bhabha (1994) describes as the "third space" a border cultural terrain in which hybrid identities are not merely imaginable but politically and socially productive. This terrain provides the site for new forms of culture, aesthetic representation, and political subjectivity that disrupt the fixity of national and ethnic identity.

Both mainstream and diasporic media representations are essential to this process of identity formation. Global flows of Bollywood cinema, Indian television, and diasporic digital media like YouTube and Instagram have facilitated the diaspora in producing affective forms of cultural consumption and belonging across spatiality (Mankekar, 2015; Rai, 2020). These media spaces create a sense of continuity with the homeland as well as provide space for re-interpreting Indian culture in forms that speak to diasporic lived realities. But the same media also work to reinforce exclusionary notions of Indianness favouring certain caste, class, and gender norms, thus excluding subaltern voices in the diaspora (Maira, 2002). As a result, diasporic media spaces are sites of conflict where identity is negotiated not just through representation but also through omission and silence.

Immigration regimes and workplaces also have a strong bearing on identity outcomes. For example, the Gulf-based segmented labour market and Southeast Asia-based segments impose social constraints upon the mobility of working-class Indian migrants, with special reference to those who toil in poorly paid sectors of employment such as construction or housework (Osella & Osella, 2012; Jureidini, 2014). These migrants endure social exclusion, precarious legality, and restricted cultural incorporation, as a result giving rise to structures of diasporic marginality different from Global North-based elite professionals. This diasporic stratification highlights the need to examine diasporic identity from an intersectional perspective that is sensitive to class, caste, gender, and legal status. The sociological point here is unmistakable: the diaspora is not a unified whole but a fractured and internally segmented formation, in which identity and belonging are mediated by relations of power both within and beyond the community (Anthias, 1998).

In addition, the legal and political infrastructures of host countries influence the options for diasporic involvement and identity formation. Immigration policies, multicultural policies, and citizenship regimes shape not just diaspora settlement patterns but also how much a sense of belonging and civic identity is experienced. In liberal multicultural nations such as Canada and the UK, diasporic communities have greater room to reclaim their cultural particularity and engagement in the public sphere, whereas in other societies, assimilationist forces or xenophobic ideologies can translate into cultural suppression or identity dilution (Soysal, 1994; Modood, 2007). Diasporic identity is here an act of resistance and resilience a strategic reclaiming of cultural autonomy in the face of homogenizing national discourses.

Punjabi Diaspora

The Punjabi diaspora, one of the most prominent and influential diasporic communities from South Asia, has played a pivotal role in shaping the socio-cultural, economic, and political landscapes of both their host countries and their homeland, India. Their migration, which spans over a century, has created a transnational network that connects Punjab to various parts of the world, including Canada, the United Kingdom, the United States, Australia, and the Middle East. This book delves into the creative efforts of the Punjabi diaspora in nation-building, examining their socio-cultural and historical contributions through a sociological lens. By analysing their transnational connections, cultural preservation, and innovative contributions, this study aims to provide a nuanced understanding of how the Punjabi diaspora has become a key agent in global and local processes of development and identity formation. The socio-economic factors influencing the Punjabi diaspora's contributions are multifaceted, encompassing historical migration patterns, economic motivations, cultural preservation, and political engagement. These factors are deeply intertwined with the diaspora's identity and their efforts to contribute to both their host countries and their homeland.

The historical context of Punjabi migration is crucial to understanding the socio-economic factors that have shaped the diaspora's contributions. The migration of Punjabis can be traced back to the colonial era when the British Empire recruited them as soldiers, labourers, and agricultural workers. The British colonial administration viewed Punjabis as a "martial race" and actively recruited them into the British Indian Army (Talbot & Thandi, 2004). This early migration laid the foundation for the Punjabi diaspora, as many soldiers and labourers settled in British colonies such as Canada, Australia, and East Africa. The partition of India in 1947 further accelerated Punjabi migration, as millions were displaced and forced to seek refuge in foreign lands. The trauma of partition, coupled with economic hardships, led to a significant outflow of Punjabis to countries such as the United Kingdom and the United States (Dusenbery & Tatla, 2009). The post-independence period saw a new wave of Punjabi migration, driven by the search for better economic opportunities and the desire to escape the socio-political challenges in Punjab. The Green Revolution of the 1960s, while transforming Punjab into the breadbasket of India, also created economic disparities and environmental degradation, prompting many to seek opportunities abroad (Thandi, 2012). Today, the Punjabi diaspora is estimated to be over 10 million people, making it one of the largest and most influential diasporic communities from South Asia.

From a sociological perspective, the Punjabi diaspora represents a unique case of cultural hybridity and transnationalism. They have managed to maintain their cultural identity while simultaneously adapting to the socio-cultural norms of their host countries. This duality is evident in their creative efforts, which range from literary works and artistic expressions to entrepreneurial ventures and philanthropic activities. These efforts are not only a means of preserving their heritage but also a way of contributing to the socio-economic development of their homeland and host nations. One of the most significant contributions of the Punjabi diaspora is their role in the cultural revival and promotion of the Punjabi language, literature, and arts. Despite being geographically dispersed, the diaspora has established numerous cultural organizations, festivals, and media outlets that celebrate Punjabi culture. For instance, the annual Punjabi International Film Festival (PIFF) in Canada and the United Kingdom showcases Punjabi cinema, providing a platform for film-makers and artists to connect with global audiences (Dhaliwal, 2018). Such initiatives not only preserve Punjabi culture but also foster a sense of unity and pride among the diaspora.

The Punjabi diaspora has also played a crucial role in the promotion of Punjabi literature. Writers such as Khushwant Singh, Amrita Pritam, and Navtej Bharati have gained international recognition for their works, which often explore themes of migration, identity, and cultural hybridity (Grewal, 2007). These literary contributions have not only enriched Punjabi literature but also provided a platform for the diaspora to engage with their cultural heritage. In addition to literature, the Punjabi diaspora has been instrumental in the global popularity of Punjabi music, particularly *Bhangra*. The rise of Punjabi artists such as Diljit Dosanjh, Jazzy B., and Gurdas Maan have brought Punjabi music to the forefront of the global stage (Sharma, 2020). This cultural export not only enhances India's soft power but also creates economic opportunities for artists and entrepreneurs in Punjab. The socio-economic impact of these cultural contributions is significant, as they generate revenue, create jobs, and promote Punjab's cultural heritage on a global scale.

The economic contributions of the Punjabi diaspora are another critical aspect of their nation-building efforts. According to the World Bank, India is the largest recipient of remittances globally, with Punjab being one of the top beneficiary states (World Bank, 2021). These remittances have significantly contributed to the state's infrastructure development, education, and healthcare sectors. For instance, many Punjabi families rely on remittances to fund their children's education, build homes, and start businesses (Thandi, 2012). The inflow of remittances has also led to the growth of the real estate sector in Punjab, as many diaspora members invest in property in their homeland. This has created a ripple effect in the local economy, generating employment opportunities and boosting economic growth. In addition to remittances, the Punjabi diaspora has also invested in various sectors in Punjab, including agriculture, manufacturing, and information technology. Many diaspora members have established businesses in Punjab, creating employment opportunities and contributing to the state's economic growth. For example, the Ludhiana-based textile industry has benefited from investments by the Punjabi diaspora, leading to the growth of small and medium-sized enterprises (SMEs) in the region (Purewal, 2019).

The entrepreneurial spirit of the Punjabi diaspora is also evident in their ventures abroad. Many Punjabi immigrants have established successful businesses in their host countries, ranging from restaurants and grocery stores to real estate and transportation companies. These businesses not only contribute to the local economy but also serve as a bridge between the diaspora and their homeland, fostering economic and cultural exchanges. The success of Punjabi entrepreneurs abroad has also inspired many in Punjab to pursue entrepreneurial ventures, leading to the growth of startups and SMEs in the region. The socio-economic impact of these entrepreneurial efforts is significant, as they create jobs, generate revenue, and contribute to the overall development of both the host countries and Punjab.

The Punjabi diaspora's philanthropic activities are another important aspect of their nation-building efforts. Many Punjabi diaspora members have established charitable organizations and foundations that focus on education, healthcare, and rural development in Punjab. For example, the Pingalwara Charitable Society, founded by Bhagat Puran Singh and supported by the diaspora, provides care for the disabled, destitute, and marginalized sections of society (Singh, 2010). Such initiatives highlight the diaspora's commitment to social justice and inclusive development. In addition to healthcare, the Punjabi diaspora has also contributed to the education sector in Punjab. Many diaspora members have established schools, colleges, and universities in Punjab, providing quality education to underprivileged students. For instance, the Punjab-based Guru Nanak Dev University has received significant funding from the Punjabi diaspora, enabling it to expand its infrastructure and academic programmes (Thandi, 2012). These educational institutions not only provide opportunities for students but also contribute to the overall development of the region.

The Punjabi diaspora has also been actively involved in rural development projects in Punjab. Many diaspora members have funded the construction of roads, bridges, and community centres in rural areas, improving the quality of life for local residents. These projects not only address the infrastructural needs of rural Punjab but also foster a sense of community and solidarity among the diaspora and their homeland. The socio-economic impact of these philanthropic efforts is significant, as they contribute to the overall development of Punjab and improve the quality of life for its residents. The diaspora's commitment to social justice and inclusive development is evident in their efforts to address the socio-economic challenges faced by Punjab, such as poverty, unemployment, and lack of access to education and healthcare.

From a historical perspective, the Punjabi diaspora's contributions to nation-building can be traced back to the pre-independence era when Punjabi migrants played a crucial role in the Indian independence movement. Figures such as Lala Lajpat Rai and Bhagat Singh, who were influenced by their diasporic experiences, became iconic leaders in the struggle for freedom (Grewal, 2007). Their contributions to the independence movement highlight the diaspora's commitment to the ideals of justice, equality, and freedom. In the post-independence period, the Punjabi diaspora continued to contribute to India's nation-building efforts through their involvement in politics, education, and social reform. Many diaspora members have held prominent positions in Indian politics, advocating for the rights and interests of Punjab and its people. For instance, Sardar Swaran Singh, a prominent Punjabi politician, played a key role in shaping India's foreign policy and economic development (Talbot & Thandi, 2004).

The Punjabi diaspora has also been actively involved in advocating for the rights of Sikhs and other minority communities in India. Many diaspora organizations, such as the Sikh Federation (UK) and the Sikh Coalition (USA), have been at the forefront of campaigns for religious freedom, human rights, and social justice (Purewal, 2019). These efforts highlight the diaspora's commitment to the ideals of democracy and equality but also contribute to the overall development of India as a pluralistic and inclusive society. The socio-economic impact of these political contributions is significant, as they promote social justice, equality, and inclusive development in India. The diaspora's efforts to advocate for the rights of minorities communities have also contributed to the overall development of Punjab, as they address the socio-political challenges faced by the region.

Despite their significant contributions, the Punjabi diaspora's engagement with Punjab is not without challenges. Issues such as cultural assimilation, identity crisis, and generational gaps pose significant obstacles to the preservation of Punjabi culture and heritage. Many second and third-generation Punjabi immigrants struggle to maintain their cultural identity in the face of globalization and cultural homogenization (Dhaliwal, 2018). This has led to a decline in the use of the Punjabi language and traditional cultural practices among the younger generation. Moreover, the diaspora's engagement with Punjab is often criticized for being limited to economic contributions, with little focus on addressing the region's socio-political issues such as drug abuse, unemployment, and environmental degradation (Purewal, 2019). While remittances and investments have contributed to Punjab's economic development, they have not necessarily translated into sustainable and inclusive growth. The lack of a holistic approach to diaspora engagement has led to a disconnect between the diaspora and the local population, with many Punjabis feeling that the diaspora is out of touch with the ground realities of the region.

To address these challenges, there is a need for a more holistic and inclusive approach to diaspora engagement. This includes not only economic contributions but also active participation in social and political reforms. The Punjabi diaspora can play a crucial role in addressing the socio-political challenges in Punjab by leveraging their resources, networks, and expertise. For instance, diaspora organizations can collaborate with local NGOs and government agencies to implement sustainable development projects that address issues such as drug abuse, unemployment, and environmental degradation. In addition, there is a need for greater cultural exchange and dialogue between the diaspora and the local population. This can be achieved through initiatives such as cultural festivals, exchange programmes, and collaborative projects that promote mutual understanding and cooperation. By fostering a sense of unity and solidarity, the Punjabi diaspora can contribute to the overall development of Punjab and India as a whole.

Drawing on the necessity for a more holistic and inclusive diaspora engagement, there is a need to examine how the identity of the Punjabi diaspora is constructed through wider sociological processes of globalization, cultural negotiation, and social reproduction. The current disconnection between the diasporic community and the national community of Punjab can be explained through the sociological prism of "long-distance nationalism" (Anderson, 1992), wherein diasporic subjects feel a symbolic and emotional connection with the homeland, but are separated from its everyday reality through physical and social distance. Although their investments and remittances substantially contribute to the economic prosperity of Punjab, their exclusion from grassroots socio-political agitation and everyday struggle tends to reinforce a commodified and romanticized Punjabi identity hyped in overseas cultural festivals but disconnected from the root concerns of the region, including youth marginalization, agrarian crisis, and caste differentials (Kaur, 2012).

In addition, younger and newer-generation diasporas often find themselves in a "third space" (Bhabha, 1994) where they constitute their identity, not out of binary home/foreign cultures, but hybridized, negotiated signification. In this intermedial or between-space place stand both risk and possibility. For one thing, it affords diaspora youths the opportunities for re-conception of Punjabi identity within the new arenas such as diaspora literature, global digitalities, and cyber-mediated activism. Conversely, it also instils a feeling of cultural ambivalence and fragmentation of identity, particularly since the younger populations will suffer from erosion of language, loss of strength in cultural rituals, and dissonant loyalties between their ethnic origins and national affiliations in their respective host lands (Baumann, 1996).

An engagement strategy rooted in sociology must hence acknowledge these cultural and generational changes. Punjab and host country institutions can create spaces for intergenerational conversation, cultural exchange, and civic cooperation. These spaces can facilitate a more reflexive mode of diaspora engagement that moves beyond symbolic affiliation to include practical solidarity. For example, diaspora organizations led by youth can co-create education and mental health programmes for rural Punjab that focus on digital access, job readiness, and drug addiction domains that are presently under-served (Grewal, 2021). Joint research between Punjabi researchers overseas and domestic universities can also produce context-specific knowledge that guides policy on rural development and sustainability.

Additionally, the theory of "diasporic development" (Gamlen, 2014) provides a framework for conceptualizing how the diaspora can be agents of change not only economically, but also politically and socially. Diasporic involvement must be institutionalized through official channels that enable representation, accountability, and strategic planning. For instance, diaspora bond policies, voting rights for Non-Resident Indians (NRIs), or advisory councils with diaspora representatives can assist in bridging the gap between diasporic hopes and domestic policy requirements (Rai, 2019). The challenge is to develop a model of co-development that is inclusive, sustainable, and based on mutual respect, as opposed to one that merely valorises diaspora capital without redressing inequalities within Punjab itself.

A key zone that is little explored is the way intersecting axes of caste, gender, and class impinge on the experiences and achievements of the diaspora. Women of the Punjabi diaspora, for example, frequently involve themselves in transnational caregiving, cultural reproduction, and communal building that are vital but poorly recognized aspects of diasporic existence (Mankekar, 2015). Likewise, *Dalit* and other lower-caste diasporic groups may be subjected to multiple exclusions, both within host countries and among upper-caste and male-dominated elite diaspora circles. Distinguishing these internal hierarchies is necessary to ensure that diaspora engagement is not merely transnational but also revolutionary.

Building upon the earlier described contributions and multifaceted involvement of the Punjabi diaspora, it is necessary to place this case in the larger context of the Indian diaspora, which offers a rich and varied ground for sociological exploration. The Indian diaspora is not a homogeneous entity but a heterogeneous construction based on regional, linguistic, caste, class, religious, and generational variations. This diversity, while offering distinct cultural expressions in different parts of the world, also offers a rich terrain to analyse larger sociological issues like identity, transnationalism, globalization, cultural reproduction, and diaspora nationalism. The everyday life of Indian diaspora communities overseas whether Punjabi, Gujarati, Tamil, Telugu, Malayali, or Bengali mimics separate patterns of migration and settlement that shape both the integration processes as well as maintaining homeland connections.

Sociologically, the Indian diaspora challenges conventional notions of the nation-state and belonging by creating what Benedict Anderson (1991) described as "imagined communities" that are located beyond national borders. These communities tend to reproduce their sense of identity through symbolic and material acts, such as the preservation of language, religion, dress, food practices, and rituals, while at the same time negotiating the needs and expectations of the host society. The active interplay between assimilation and cultural maintenance is seen in day-to-day practices, and also in diasporic institutions like temples, *gurdwaras*, mosques, community centres, ethnic businesses, and media networks (Clifford, 1994). They not only provide places of community formation but also serve as cultural anchors mediating the relationship between the diaspora and the homeland.

One of the central ideas of diaspora research is transnationalism, meaning the sustenance of various forms of connections social, economic, political, and affective between nation-states (Basch, Glick Schiller, & Szanton Blanc, 1994). Indian diaspora members actively engage in transnational activities such as sending remittances, political activism, charity, and cultural reproduction and thus shape their host nations and countries of origin. For example, the extensive Gujarati business communities in East Africa and the UK have been practicing philanthropy through the construction of schools, hospitals, and religious centres in their villages of origin in India, illustrating the manner in which cultural values and capital flow across borders (Brah, 1996). Likewise, Indian diaspora communities in the United States have served important roles in influencing pro-immigrant immigration policies and constructing soft power for India by advancing Indian culture and tradition, particularly through Bollywood, *yoga*, and classical music.

The power of the diaspora over the Indian state's policy agenda has also grown more visible over the past few decades. The Indian Government has institutionalized its engagement with the diaspora through programmes like the Pravasi Bharatiya Divas, Overseas Citizen of India (OCI) status, and the Ministry of External Affairs' Division of Overseas Indian Affairs. These programmes are indicative of the state's appreciation of the diaspora as a national development resource, particularly in the areas of foreign direct investment, knowledge transfer, and cultural diplomacy (Varadarajan, 2010). The diaspora's contribution to India's growth has also become symbolic, with stories of diasporic achievement being highlighted in national media in order to project a vision of a successful India on the world stage. This is part of the creation of what sociologist S. Shankar (2015) terms "diaspora nationalism", where the nation is imagined as transnational success and affective allegiance rather than territoriality.

Within the sphere of identity, the Indian diaspora provides us with crucial insights into the formation of hybrid subjectivities. According to Homi Bhabha (1994), cultural identities are created in the "third space" of enunciation, where the negotiation between the cultural codes of the homeland and the host society creates new forms of belonging. Diasporic identities are fluid rather than static and are instead dynamic and contextual, determined by generation, class, gender, and the host country's socio-political climate. Strong attachments to India and cultural identification with language, religion, and customs are typical for first-generation migrants. Second- and third-generation diaspora individuals, however, often have to negotiate dual or multiple identities, at times encountering identity crises or issues of authenticity. This generation change is usually characterized by a transition from nostalgia-based cultural reproduction to more selective and innovative uses of Indian culture, for example, fusion music, diasporic writing, and South Asian youth subcultures (Desai, 2004; Maira, 2002).

Gender is also a key aspect in the sociological understanding of the Indian diaspora. Indian women's experiences in diaspora differ greatly depending on their migration mode, class, and region of origin. While some women have migrated as dependents within family-based migration systems, others have become independent migrants, professionals, or entrepreneurs. The diaspora tends to reproduce patriarchal gender norms but also creates spaces for the renegotiation of gender roles. For instance, in some diaspora settings, Indian women have discovered education and work opportunities that might have been denied them in their home country, resulting in new modes of agency and empowerment (Bhachu, 1985). Nevertheless, issues like domestic violence, cultural policing, and the responsibility of maintaining "authentic" cultural values in foreign settings also continue to exist (Dasgupta, 1998).

Religion is a major axis of cohesion and differentiation in the Indian diaspora. Diasporic Hinduism, Sikhism, Islam, Christianity, and Jainism have all assumed distinct forms in host nations, frequently responding to the imperatives of multiculturalism and secularism in Western liberal democracies. Temples, *gurdwaras*, and mosques are not only religious centres but also cultural and community centres that impart values, language, and identity from generation to generation. The religious revivalism found among most diaspora communities both reflects a reaction to marginalization and an effort to establish moral moorings in distant lands. Simultaneously, inter-religious dynamics, caste distinctions, and sectarian politics can be rearticulated within diasporic contexts, occasionally resonating with the communal tensions of the homeland (Kurien, 2007; Jakobsh, 2006).

The cultural productions of the Indian diaspora literature, film, music, and visual arts are yet another significant space in which diasporic identities are negotiated and represented. Authors like Salman Rushdie, Jhumpa Lahiri, and Bharati Mukherjee have engaged with themes of displacement, hybridity, and yearning in their writing, providing nuanced insights into the diasporic condition. Diasporic film, especially films made in the UK, US, and Canada, like "Bend It Like Beckham" or "The

Namesake", represent the daily tensions of bicultural identity, intergenerational conflict, and the negotiation of gender roles (Gopinath, 2005). These cultural texts not only represent diasporic experiences but also actively construct how diasporic communities imagine themselves and are imagined by others.

Notably, the Indian diaspora is also stratified socio-economically, with considerable differences in capital, mobility, and integration. While highly skilled professional diaspora, especially in the United States and Western Europe, are mostly glorified for their prosperity and boosting India's image worldwide, there is a sizeable part of the Indian diaspora employed under exploitative conditions in countries such as the Gulf, Southeast Asia, and some parts of Africa. These migrants typically experience exploitative labour conditions, legal precariousness, and restricted access to rights. Sociologically, this makes it important to examine the diaspora not merely in terms of celebration but also in terms of labour, exploitation, and class (Rodrigues, 2017). The uneven deployment of mobility and capital within the Indian diaspora complicates celebratory accounts of success and demands a more intersectional, critical understanding.

Overall, then, the Indian diaspora, with all its disparate interactions with the host societies and the homeland, offers a rich ground for sociological analysis. Its richness lies not only in its enormity or geographic extent but in the varied manners in which it has restructured ideas about identity, community, nation, and belonging. Through both local and global, traditional and contemporary, the Indian diaspora is both a mirror and a motor for change in the modern world.

2

Reviews

For the present study some literature reviews are important because it identify the key scholarly debates theoretical gaps, and imperical patterns surrounding migration and diaspora engagement. It also help to establish the need of further research in this area.

1. Aziz *et al.* (2023), examine the interaction between migration and interprovincial trade in Canada, modelling the economic effects of provincial migration and immigration based on a gravity model framework. The research employs different econometric estimators, such as pooled OLS, fixed effects, and instrumental variable techniques, to investigate the link between migration flows and interprovincial trade. Evidence shows that both immigration and provincial migration improve trade, especially imports, but immigrants have a greater contribution to international trade than interprovincial trade because of their limited knowledge of Canadian provinces. Also, common language and openness to trade ease trade, while distance in geography is a hindrance. The research identifies structural constraints that inhibit full integration of migrants into provincial economies, solidifying regional imbalances.

Provincial protectionism and inconsistent regulation, according to the findings, ensure perpetuation of economic disparities, confining the growth potential of migration-driven trade. Though economic efficiency is prioritized in the research, social and cultural aspects of migration, e.g., the contribution of migrant communities towards building cohesion and crossing cultural boundaries, are neglected. To fully leverage migration's benefits, Canada must adopt policies that address both economic and social integration, ensuring equitable development across provinces.

2. Singh (2023) analyses the increasing tensions between Canada and India with a focus on the revival of Sikh separatism and its consequences for bilateral relations. The article places the historical origins of the Khalistan movement in context, emphasizing its revival among the Sikh diaspora, especially in Canada. Singh writes about the assassination of Hardeep Singh Nijjar, a Canadian Sikh separatist leader, and the resulting diplomatic tensions, such as mutual expulsions of diplomats and increased rhetoric between the two countries. One of the key strengths of Singh's analysis is the detailed account of the evolution of the Khalistan movement and its transnational character. The article successfully demonstrates how diaspora communities can shape homeland politics, highlighting the intricacies of identity, nationalism, and global diplomacy. Singh also discusses the dilemma of Western governments in reconciling domestic security issues with foreign policy interests, particularly in multicultural societies. The article might be improved by a more detailed analysis of the internal dynamics of the Sikh diaspora, including differences in political participation across generations and differing views on separatism. Also, as the article gives a historical context, a more in-depth analysis of the contemporary socio-political conditions that are fueling the revival of the movement would add to its pertinence to today's

world. Overall, Singh (2023) gives a relevant and insightful account of the revived Sikh separatist feelings and their effect on Canada-India relations. The paper is an important contribution to knowledge for researchers and policymakers who are studying diaspora politics, transnational movements, and global relations.

3. Kumari (2023) examines the lived experience of the Punjabi diaspora from a literary perspective, presenting selected short stories of the anthology *Punjabi Parvasian Dian Kahanian* to provide a rich account of migration, identity, and socio-cultural displacement. Engaging the affective aspects of migration, with a specific focus on the tension between nostalgia and accommodation, the study highlights literature as a potent tool of chronicling the migrant experience of alienation, marginalization, and cultural hybridity. One of the main strengths of the article is its interdisciplinary methodology combining literary analysis with sociological insight. She illustrates how diaspora writing acts as a cultural memory, retaining the affective and historical recollection of Punjabi migrants. The critique reveals how characters within the narratives navigate their identities in the midst of foreign cultural environments while maintaining strong affinities for their origins. Such double consciousness, as conceptualized in the study, is congruent with classical diaspora and transnational theories. But whereas the article shines in terms of descriptive analysis, it sometimes falls short of critical engagement with wider sociological structures like Bhabha's theory of the "third space" or Hall's theories of cultural identity. The over-reliance on textual interpretation without further wide contextualization of diasporic politics or economic aspects restricts the range of the study. Comparative diasporic accounts could have enriched analysis more. However, she makes a valuable contribution to understanding the ways in which the creative works of the Punjabi diaspora serve as instruments of meaning-making and cultural continuity. The

book opens up spaces for interdisciplinary scholarship cutting across sociology, literature, and migration studies and is therefore a useful text for scholars analyzing diasporic resilience and cultural production.

4. Archary (2022) examines the cultural heritage and transformation of Indian indentured labourers in South Africa, focusing on the life of Mrs. T.M. Singh, a widow in colonial Natal. The study highlights how culture, as a transmission of human conduct, was adapted but not erased by indentured Indians, who preserved tangible and intangible heritage through religious rituals, oral traditions, and community engagement. He emphasizes the role of migration in reshaping gender roles, religious practices, and economic activities, with women like Mrs. Singh challenging traditional patriarchy by engaging in financial decision-making. Despite colonial oppression, Indian cultural heritage demonstrated resilience through adaptive transformation, as seen in the evolution of practices like prayer times dictated by labour schedules. The research critiques the concept of de-acculturalization, arguing that migration fostered hybrid identities rather than cultural erasure. However, the reliance on oral history raises concerns about subjectivity and selective memory. He contributes to broader sociological discussions on cultural resilience, social stratification, and gendered agency in migration studies, while calling for comparative analyses with other indentured diaspora to strengthen findings. This study underscores the complexities of identity formation in post-colonial societies, offering critical insights into the interplay of cultural preservation and transformation under systemic oppression.

5. Farhat and Rather (2020) examine the trade relationship between India and the UAE using the Trade Intensity Index (TII), a quantitative tool introduced by Kojima to measure bilateral trade dynamics. The study reveals a declining trend in India's

export intensity to the UAE, from 12.5 in 2001 to 6.6 in 2016, attributed to reduced exports of textiles, cereals, and aircraft parts. Conversely, India's import intensity remained stable, with minor fluctuations between 2.14 and 5.0, reflecting a consistent reliance on UAE's petroleum and precious stones. The authors conclude that while India-UAE trade remains robust, both nations must diversify their trade portfolios to sustain economic cooperation. From a sociological perspective, the study's reliance on quantitative metrics overlooks the lived experiences of Indian migrant workers in the UAE, who contribute significantly to remittances but often face precarious labour conditions. The analysis also neglects the socio-economic implications of trade dependency, such as the reinforcement of extractive industries and the lack of diversification in labour-intensive sectors. Furthermore, the study does not address how global economic shifts, such as the 2010 financial crisis, disproportionately affect working-class communities. A more holistic approach, integrating labour rights, migration patterns, and socio-political dynamics, would provide a deeper understanding of the India-UAE trade relationship beyond economic metrics.

6. Singh (2017) provides a close reading of diasporic Punjabi short fiction as a literary site for the articulation of migrant consciousness. The article examines the manner in which tropes of displacement, cultural dissonance, struggles of identity, and nostalgia are carefully interwoven in present-day Parvasi fiction. Singh points out how such narratives are representations of emotional and ideological prolongations of migration—largely defined by a lack of roots and a search for belonging. One of the article's strengths is its focus on the emotional and psychological aspects of migration. The author highlights repeating themes of alienation, intergenerational conflict, and conflict between tradition and modernity. These are well employed to illustrate how literary fiction captures the internal space of diasporic

individuals. The article could use a more robust theoretical framework. The lack of engagement with notable diaspora theorists or models restricts the level of analysis. Moreover, the research is mostly descriptive in nature, and greater comparative or intersectional analysis might further establish its sociological significance. With these caveats aside, Singh (2017) manages to highlight the significance of literature in expressing the migrant psyche and upholding cultural memory, which makes it an important text for scholarship on cultural expression among diaspora communities.

7. Alam and Ahmed (2018) examine the changing trade relationship between India and the Gulf Cooperation Council (GCC) through the lens of an extended gravity model, capturing the economic and socio-political aspects of such a relationship. They draw upon the literature on international trade, regionalism, and the economics of migration, stressing the trend towards bilateral and regional trade agreements in the context of stunted multilateral world trade negotiations. Previous literature on India-GCC trade highlights the importance of oil imports and labour remittances, adding to India's trade deficit and economic dependence on the region. The analysis fits into gravity model-based explanations of determinants of trade with variables like GDP, trade openness, and socio-cultural relations that have long been established as key factors in trade flows. Yet, the literature also criticizes the gravity model's inability to capture socio-political factors, including labour rights and migration policies, that strongly influence India-GCC relations. Researchers have argued over the trade-offs between economic gains and migrant vulnerabilities, with research showing that remittances support India's economy while perpetuating socio-economic inequalities. Alam and Ahmed's work adds to this discussion by recognizing the untapped trade potential while also warning against a too econometric approach that fails to consider

the human cost of labour migration. Their results emphasize the importance of integrated policy regimes that address both trade liberalization and migrant welfare.

8. Roy (2014) offers a strong and nuanced narrative of the Punjabi diaspora, critically analyzing how imaginaries of Punjab have developed over more than a century of migration. Placing her analysis within the larger field of diaspora studies, Roy examines how Punjabi identity, culture, and memory are constantly remade and reimagined in transnational spaces. The article provides a theoretical framing that aligns with cultural studies and diaspora theory, particularly focusing on the interplay between memory, homeland, and cultural reproduction. One of the notable strengths of Roy's work is its historical breadth. By tracing Punjabi migration from the late 19th century to contemporary times, she highlights the dynamic and heterogeneous nature of diasporic experiences. The article provides an understanding of how waves of migrants have influenced the cultural and political discourses of Punjab from a distance, via media, literature, music, and political activism. Critically, although the article is conceptually dense, it is also somewhat abstract and general in places, without empirical evidence or case-specific examples that could have anchored the discussion. Roy alludes to multiple creative and political practices among the diaspora without investigating them extensively. A further analysis of gender, class, or regional differences within the Punjabi diaspora would have enhanced the analysis. However, there is a notable contribution by Roy (2014) in terms of placing the Punjabi diaspora not merely as a transnational community of exile but an active agent influencing the cultural and historical awareness of both the homelands as well as host countries. This article is a rich academic study to learn how the cultural politics of diaspora identity formation gets constructed in our globalized times.

9. Chanda and Ghosh (2013) offer a detailed socio-economic overview of the Punjabi diaspora in the UK with a focus on their transnational links and complex contributions to India. The report succinctly emphasizes the contribution of remittances, philanthropic activities, knowledge transfers, and investments in infrastructure and education, particularly in Punjab. This research provides rich empirical data and historical context, rendering it a key resource for navigating the diaspora's place in India's development story. One of the report's greatest strengths is its sociologically grounded approach, analyzing migration dynamics, community formation, and identity politics. It also probes how diasporic involvement is shaped by changing generations, immigration policies, and socio-political changes in India and the UK. Nevertheless, even though the report offers a lush descriptive narrative, it could have been improved through more substantive theoretical grounding. Issues such as transnationalism, cultural hybridity, or nationalism in diaspora are not pushed to their extent, and so the analytical range is constrained. In addition, the research keeps generalizing Punjabi diaspora without fully substantiating internal variations based on caste, class, or religious groups. Nevertheless, Chanda and Ghosh (2013) make a valuable contribution by recording how the Punjabi diaspora plays a bridging role between countries, innovative engagement in India's nation-building remotely.

10. Niumai (2011) in his study of Indian diaspora philanthropy, as a sociological phenomenon, intersects economic, cultural, and religious dimensions, yet remains underexplored in its systemic implications. Existing literature reveals that Non-Resident Indians (NRIs) and Persons of Indian Origin (PIOs) engage in philanthropy through formal and informal channels, often shaped by kinship, caste, and religious affiliations. Elite organizations like the American Association of Physicians of Indian Origin (AAPI) and the Asian American Hotel Owners

Association (AAHOA) play pivotal roles in mobilizing resources for healthcare, education, and disaster relief in India, reflecting the influence of class and power dynamics. Historically rooted in religious traditions, Indian philanthropy was institutionalized by figures like Gandhi for social reform, yet contemporary practices often reinforce socio-economic hierarchies, favouring elite institutions over grassroots development. The evolution of the Indian American diaspora, from early labour migrants to a highly skilled "model minority", underscores the role of post-1965 immigration reforms and India's economic liberalization in wealth accumulation. However, the "model minority" narrative obscures socio-economic disparities and critiques how philanthropy serves as a tool for elite influence. The rise of media and technology has expanded participation through online donations, yet issues of transparency, political influence, and U.S. anti-terrorism policies complicate international giving. Critically, reliance on diaspora philanthropy as a substitute for state welfare risks perpetuating inequalities, highlighting the need for inclusive, equitable approaches. Future research must interrogate whether diaspora giving fosters genuine social progress or entrenches existing power structures.

3

Research Methodology

Sociological research methodology is more than an aggregation of techniques; it is a procedural and philosophical structure that guides how sociologists study human action, social organization, and cultural processes. It acts as a mediator between empirical inquiry and theoretical understanding, affecting the manner in which researchers frame questions, interpret findings, and develop social knowledge (Bourdieu, 1990). Methodology gives sociology its distinctive identity by ensuring that research is rigorous, ethical, and reflexive. It also demands awareness of the ontological and epistemological assumptions inherent in different research traditions, whether they seek to explain social regularities, interpret human meanings, or resist power relations (Bhaskar, 1975; Horkheimer & Adorno, 2002).

At the core of sociological methodology are competing paradigms that guide research design. Positivist approaches, rooted in Comte's (1853) definition of sociology as a science, maintain objectivity, measurement, and causal explanation. These methodologies are more likely to employ large scale questionnaires, statistical methods, and experiments to hunt for patterns and check hypotheses (Campbell & Stanley, 2015;

Babbie, 2016). Interpretivist methodologies, citing Weber (1978) and Schutz (1967), are focused on meaning-making and subjectivity and employ qualitative methods like ethnography, in-depth interviews, and discourse analysis to capture lived experience (Bryman, 2016; Neuman, 2014). Critical traditions, with their roots in feminist and Marxist philosophy, object to how research can entrench social inequalities, advocating participatory action research and emancipatory methods that prioritize marginal voices (Smith, 1987), Creswell & Creswell, 2023).

Methodological integrity depends on thoughtful selection of study methods in consonance with research purpose. Quantitative methods, such as secondary data analysis and surveys, provide generalizable trends and correlation results that offer a macro level understanding of social phenomena (Smith, 2018). Quantitative methods may, however, lack the depth of human experience, and qualitative methods are crafted to compensate for these limitations. For example, ethnographic research places the researcher in the field among communities to observe cultural practices and social interactions as they naturally happen (Neuman, 2014). Case studies, narrative analysis, and phenomenology also enable sociologists to explore the depth and richness of individual and group experience (Merleau-Ponty, 1962). Mixed-methods research more and more blends quantitative and qualitative approaches, integrating statistical data with ethnographic insight to provide a better understanding of social issues (Creswell & Creswell, 2023).

Ethical considerations lie at the centre of sociological research methodology, demanding that studies preserve respect for the rights and well-being of participants. Institutional review boards apply ethical principles such as informed consent, privacy, and minimization of harm (ASA, 2019). Reflexivity is also vital, with researchers required to acknowledge their own bias, positions in society, and the influence they have on the research process (Gouldner, 1970). As sociologists belong to the social world they study, self-knowledge enhances methodological accountability and transparency. Ethical matters, such as how to manage power relations during fieldwork or represent oppressed groups without stereotyping, require continual ethical practice (Smith, 1987).

Sociological research practice similarly connects theory and practice, determining how researchers make sense of data and construct knowledge. Critical realism, for instance, acknowledges structural determinism as well as the agency of people, demanding that research expose underlying social mechanisms (Bhaskar, 1975). Phenomenology focuses on personal consciousness and lived experience, emphasizing how people construct meaning in everyday life (Merleau-Ponty, 1962). Methodological choices reflect broader theoretical stances, whether a research study seeks to describe economic inequalities, investigate identity formation, or promote social justice. For example, a research study of labour exploitation might use statistical analysis to measure wage disparities while supplementing with ethnographic descriptions to portray workers' everyday lives (Creswell & Creswell, 2023).

Methodological innovation is essential in contemporary sociology to counteract new challenges introduced by globalization, digitalization, and technological change. Online interactions are analysed through digital ethnography, while big data analysis reveals social patterns on a scale previously unknown (Smith, 2018). These innovations bring new ethical and methodological concerns, such as data privacy concerns and the application of artificial intelligence in social research. Without methodological depth, sociology runs the danger of being empiricist amassing facts with little interpretation or overly abstracted, divorced from everyday life (Bourdieu, 1990).

Sociological research methodology is a reflexive and adaptive practice that modifies itself in tandem with society. It requires researchers to critically engage philosophical debates, moral dilemmas, and emerging social transformations. Through theory, method, and reflexivity, sociologists create science that is both scientifically rigorous as well as socially meaningful, contributing to scholarship at the academic as well as to social change. With a more complex world, methodological excellence remains at the core of sociology, ensuring research continues to enlighten, problematize, and revolutionize human societies.

Research Gap

The existing literature on the Punjabi diaspora provides a robust foundation for understanding their socio-cultural, economic, and political contributions to nation-building. Scholars such as Niumai (2011), Archary (2022), Parry (2021), Alam and Ahmed (2018), Aziz *et al.* (2023), and Farhat and Rather (2020) have explored various dimensions of diaspora engagement, including philanthropy, cultural preservation, economic contributions, and political advocacy. However, while these studies offer valuable insights, they often operate in silos, focusing on specific aspects of diaspora contributions without adequately addressing the intersectionality of these dimensions. For instance, Niumai (2011) critiques the role of elite philanthropy in reinforcing socio-economic hierarchies, but does not explore how caste, class, and gender intersect to shape these dynamics. Similarly, Archary (2022) highlights the agency of women in reshaping gender roles among indentured labourers, but does not extend this analysis to contemporary Punjabi women in the diaspora. Parry (2021) discusses the political contributions of Indian Americans, but does not examine how these contributions influence socio-political dynamics in Punjab. These gaps in the literature limit our understanding of the systemic implications of diaspora contributions and their impact on both host countries and the homeland.

One of the most significant gaps in the literature is the limited exploration of the gendered dimensions of the Punjabi diaspora's contributions. While Archary (2022) provides a historical perspective on the role of women in challenging traditional patriarchy, there is a lack of contemporary research on how Punjabi women in the diaspora navigate the dual pressures of preserving cultural traditions and adapting to the socio-cultural norms of their host countries. For example, how do Punjabi women contribute to philanthropic activities, cultural preservation, and economic development? What challenges do they face in balancing their roles as cultural custodians and economic contributors? Addressing these questions would provide a more inclusive understanding of the diaspora's contributions and highlight the agency of women in shaping transnational networks and nation-building efforts.

Another critical gap is the lack of focus on intergenerational dynamics within the Punjabi diaspora. While Dhaliwal (2018) acknowledges the challenges of cultural assimilation and identity crisis among second and third-generation immigrants, there is limited research on how these dynamics influence their engagement with Punjab and their contributions to nation-building. For instance, how do younger generations perceive their cultural heritage, and what strategies do they employ to maintain their connection to Punjab? How do intergenerational differences impact the diaspora's philanthropic and entrepreneurial activities? Exploring these questions would shed light on the evolving nature of diaspora engagement and its implications for the future of nation-building.

Additionally, the literature often overlooks the role of caste and class in shaping the diaspora's contributions. While Niumai (2011) critiques how philanthropy reinforces socio-economic hierarchies, there is limited research on how caste and class dynamics influence the diaspora's engagement with Punjab. For example, how do caste affiliations shape the diaspora's philanthropic priorities and the distribution of resources? How do class differences impact the diaspora's economic contributions and their access to transnational networks? Addressing these questions would provide a more nuanced understanding of the systemic inequalities that underpin diaspora contributions and their implications for inclusive development.

Finally, there is a need for more research on the socio-political implications of the diaspora's engagement with Punjab. While Parry (2021) discusses the political contributions of Indian Americans, there is limited research on how the Punjabi diaspora's political engagement influences socio-political dynamics in Punjab. For example, how do diaspora organizations advocate for socio-political reforms in Punjab, and what impact do their efforts have on local governance and development? How do the diaspora's political contributions intersect with issues such as drug abuse, unemployment, and environmental degradation in Punjab? Exploring these questions would provide a deeper understanding of the diaspora's role in addressing the socio-political challenges faced by Punjab and their implications for sustainable development.

The existing literature on the Punjabi diaspora and their contributions to nation-building, while comprehensive, lacks a critical examination of the intersectionality of socio-cultural, economic, and political dimensions. Specifically, there is a need for more research on the gendered dimensions of diaspora contributions, particularly the role of Punjabi women in navigating cultural preservation and economic adaptation. Additionally, the intergenerational dynamics within the diaspora remain underexplored, with a limited understanding of how younger generations perceive their cultural heritage and contribute to nation-building. The role of caste and class in shaping diaspora engagement is another critical gap, as the literature often overlooks how these factors influence philanthropic priorities, economic contributions, and access to transnational networks. Finally, there is a need for more research on the socio-political implications of the diaspora's engagement with Punjab, particularly how their political contributions intersect with local governance and development challenges. Addressing these gaps would provide a more nuanced understanding of the systemic implications of diaspora contributions and their impact on both host countries and the homeland.

Objectives

- To analyze the intersectionality of socio-cultural, economic, and political factors in diaspora contributions.
- To study intergenerational dynamics and their effect on cultural heritage and nation-building.
- To investigate the influence of cultural preservation and innovation in the development of Punjab's global identity.
- To analyze the impact of transnational networks on Punjab's socio-economic progress.
- To analyze the socio-political influence of the diaspora in promoting reforms and solving governance issues in Punjab.

Area of Study

Punjab, one of the northern Indian states, is located geographically between latitudes 29.30°N to 32.32°N and longitudes 73.55°E to 76.50°E. Its northern border is with Jammu and Kashmir, and its eastern border is with Himachal Pradesh. Haryana and Rajasthan constitute its southern border, and to the west,

Punjab has an international border with Pakistan (Government of Punjab, 2023). The state is approximately 50,362 square kilometers in area and is administratively divided into 23 districts with Chandigarh as its capital (District Census Handbook, 2021). Punjab's topography is essentially an alluvial plain that is highly irrigated by the Indus river system, comprised of the Sutlej, Beas, and Ravi rivers, and which largely forms the basis of its agrarian economy.

The history of Punjab is strongly woven with ancient civilizations, invasions, and cultural changes. The area was inhabited by the Indus Valley Civilization (c. 3300-1300 BCE), with significant archaeological sites like Harappa (now in Pakistan) suggesting early urban occupation and sophisticated societal organization (Possehl, 2002). In the Vedic era (c. 1500-500 BCE), Punjab was known as the "Sapta Sindhu" or the land of seven rivers and was instrumental in the development of early Indo-Aryan society. The area experienced successive waves of invasions, starting with Darius I's Persian conquest during the 6th century BCE, followed by Alexander the Great in 326 BCE, whose battle with King Porus along the Jhelum river is well recorded (Thapar, 2004).

The following centuries saw Punjab as a battleground of choice for several empires, such as the Mauryas, Kushans, and Guptas. The propagation of Buddhism and Jainism under the Mauryan domination (4th-2nd century BCE) had a profound impact on the socio-religious texture of the area (District Gazetteer, 2019). In the medieval era, Punjab emerged as the centre of Islamic raids, starting with Mahmud of Ghazni in the 11th century and followed by the founding of Delhi Sultanate and Mughal Empire (Singh, 2018). The 16th and 15th centuries saw a great change with the rise of Sikhism, which was established by Guru Nanak Dev Ji. The Sikh Gurus contributed to the pivotal formation of the socio-political profile of Punjab, particularly during Guru Gobind Singh's reign, when the Khalsa was institutionalized in 1699. It also witnessed the establishment of the Sikh Misls and eventually the Sikh Empire by Maharaja Ranjit Singh (1799-1839), which retained its independence until annexed by the British in 1849 (Grewal, 1998).

After independence, Punjab experienced significant territorial reorganization through the Punjab Reorganization Act of 1966, which led to the creation of Haryana and Himachal Pradesh as independent states. The late 1960s' Green Revolution further solidified Punjab's position as the "Granary of India", transforming its agricultural economy (Government of India, 2022). Punjab's trajectory over time reflects its strategic and cultural importance from antiquity to the current time. Its geographical location has been a key point for migrations and invasions, which have greatly influenced its rich and varied history. For scholars, Punjab provides a platform of study that covers archaeology, history, religious changes, and agrarian evolution.

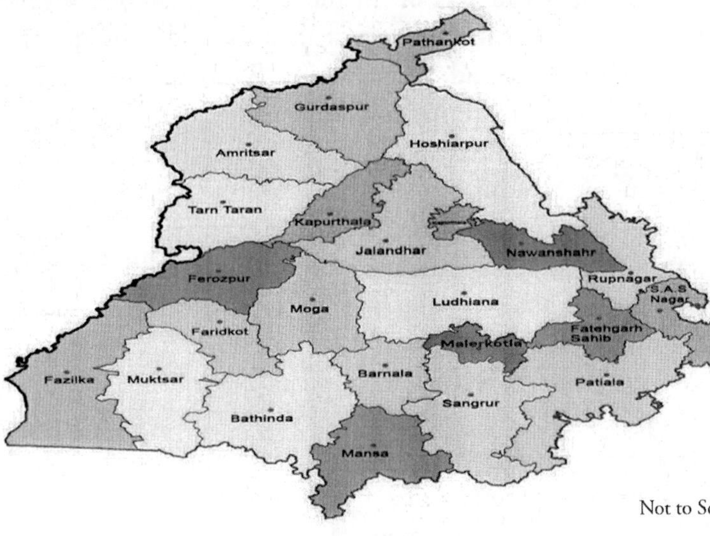

Not to Scale

Fig. 3.1

Source: https://punjab.gov.in/government/districts-of-punjab/

In order to understand the Punjabi Diaspora and their Creative Efforts for Nation Building. The present study carried out in three districts of Punjab, India which include Bathinda, Barnala and Jalandhar.

Bathinda

Bathinda, which lies in southern Punjab in the Malwa area, is a strategic and cultural region. Its geographical coordinates from 29°33′ to 30°36′ North latitude and 74°38′ to 75°46′ East longitude make it a significant node of southern Punjab with Haryana in the south and many key districts of Punjab like Sangrur, Mansa, Moga, Faridkot, and Muktsar. Its entire area is 3,353 square kilometers in size with a population density of 414 people per square kilometer, representing moderate urbanization and development compared to Punjab's average (Bathinda District Profile, Government of Punjab, n.d.; Census 2011).

Historically speaking, Bathinda's importance dates back several centuries. It has been under the control of several dynasties such as the Mauryas, Kushans, and subsequently the Delhi Sultanate and Mughals. The Bathinda Fort, or Qila Mubarak, is a testament to this complex history. It is thought to have been constructed by King Kanishka around 90-110 A.D. and was used as a military fort and administrative headquarters. It was later historically significant during the time of Razia Sultan, the first and only female ruler of the Delhi Sultanate, who was imprisoned there in the 13th century (Punjab Tourism, n.d.). The strategic location of Bathinda made it a gateway for trade and invasions, helping to shape its political and economic development over the centuries. Sociologically, Bathinda replicates the general demographic trends of Punjab, though with some local variants. As per the 2011 Census, the population was 13,88,525 with a gender imbalance of 868 females to 1,000 males, lower than the national figure of 943. This indicates ongoing gender disparities, usually due to social and cultural considerations, notwithstanding increases in literacy and awareness. The literacy level of 68.28 percent is relatively high, but there is a high gender divide male literacy of 73.79 percent and female literacy of 61.94 percent reflecting persistent issues with the education and empowerment of women (Census 2011, Government of India). Religion-wise, Bathinda continues to be a microcosm of the spiritual fabric of Punjab. Most of the people are Sikh (70.89%), reflecting the prevailing religious identity of the Malwa belt. 27.41 percent of the population is Hindu and a minority consists of Muslims (1.17%), with Christians and other religions occupying negligible percentages. This religious demography adds to the pluralistic social texture of the district, though Sikhism has all-encompassing cultural and political dominance within the region. Sikh institutions, *Gurudwaras*, and festivals form the centerpiece of public and cultural life in Bathinda (Census 2011, Government of India). Economically and socially, Bathinda is also known for its agrarian origin, supplemented in the last few decades by industrialization and power projects. Its two large thermal power plants, a fertilizer factory, and an oil refinery are a reflection of its expanding industrial base. This combination of industry and agriculture has changed the social fabric, with rising urban migration and occupational diversification, particularly among the younger generation. Yet, this development has come at a cost of pollution, water shortages, and rural-urban disparities affecting social equity and resource access (Bathinda District Industrial Profile, Ministry of MSME, Government of India, 2020). Bathinda is, therefore, an ever-changing combination of historical heritage, religious diversity, and changing socio-economic fabric. Although it has its roots in the traditional agrarian culture of Punjab, the district is also evolving towards an industrial and urban society, characterized by population changes, gender imbalance, and resultant infrastructural growth. Increased investment in education, health, and equitable growth is critical to the process of ensuring that growth benefits are transferred to the diverse constituents.

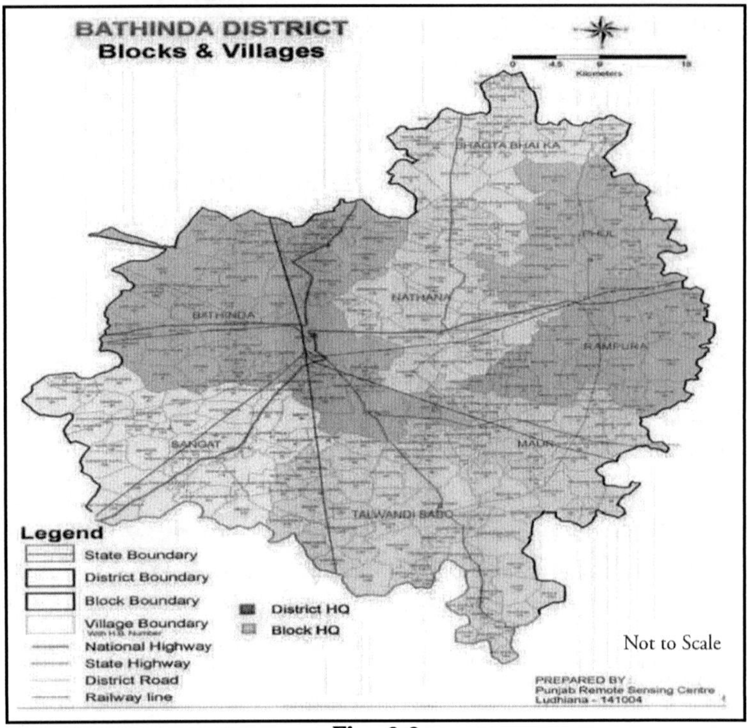

Fig. 3.2

Source: https://www.yumpu.com/xx/document/view/38070594/bathinda

Barnala

Barnala, situated centrally in Punjab, is an important geographical area as a link between the Doaba and Malwa areas. With an extent of 1,482 square kilometers, the district is bordered by Ludhiana in the north, Moga in the north-west, Bathinda in the west, and Sangrur on the other three sides. It has a population density of

402 people per square kilometer (according to the 2011 Census) and captures a semi-urban nature falling in between rural farm-based settlements and burgeoning urban enclaves (Census 2011, Government of India; barnala.gov.in). Traditionally, Barnala has played an important role in Punjab's princely and political history. It was earlier part of the Patiala princely state and even for a short duration its capital. The political awareness of the region was also demonstrated during the Indian freedom movement, more specifically through its participation in the Praja Mandal movement a people's resistance movement against princely autocracy. One such prominent regional leader was Sardar Sewa Singh Thikriwala, who spearheaded the Akali movement and challenged colonialism and princely repression. His activism generated political awareness and social reform within rural Punjab (Barnala District Administration, n.d.). The formal designation of Barnala as a distinct district was relatively new November 19, 2006 when it was separated from Sangrur district. The governmental restructuring was part of an effort to enhance governance and decentralize public services within the area (barnala.gov.in).

Sociologically, Barnala reflects the demographic profile common in Punjab's Malwa belt but with its own uniqueness. In the 2011 Census, the district counted 5,95,527 people. The sex ratio was 876 women per 1,000 men reflecting a gender imbalance, though somewhat improved over that of Bathinda. This population skew is of concern and mirrors wider societal factors of son preference, female feticide, and restricted healthcare access for women in rural areas of Punjab. Literacy levels in Barnala were reported at 67.82 percent, male literacy at 71.57 percent, and female literacy at 63.57 percent, pointing to an enduring gender divide in educational levels. Although these rates indicate an improvement from past decades, they still reflect institutional disparities in education and resource access, particularly for girls in rural families (Census 2011, Government of India).

Religiously, Barnala is predominantly Sikh with 78.54 percent population following Sikhism. This religious majority largely determines the cultural, spiritual, and political life of the district. *Gurudwaras* are not only places of worship but also social centres that foster community solidarity through practices such as *langar* (community kitchen), *sewa* (voluntary service), and collective decision-making through the *panchayat* system. The Hindu community includes 18.95 percent, Muslims 2.20 percent, and the rest is comprised of Christians and other small religions. The presence of religious diversity, though less than in urban areas such as Jalandhar, lends support to a pluralistic ethos in which religious coexistence is relatively peaceful (Census 2011, Government of India).

The district also has a robust agrarian economy, with agriculture being the primary livelihood for most of its people. The rich soil and assured irrigation through the Bhakra canal system have supported the cultivation of wheat, paddy, cotton, and maize. The agricultural base has traditionally shaped social organization and labour relations in the area. Nevertheless, as in much of rural Punjab, Barnala is subject to problems of soil degradation, falling groundwater levels, and farmer indebtedness problems that converge economic and social aspects of rural existence.

Barnala's town centre is slowly developing with small industries, particularly in cycle parts, textile weaving units, and garment production, that generate employment. These economic developments have produced a gradual but perceptible change in the sociological composition of the district. Migration, mainly by the youth, both to Indian metropolitan towns as well as overseas (particularly Canada and the UK), has brought with it new hopes, lifestyles, and remittance-based family economies. This, in turn, influences family life, gender roles, and education priorities since many families spend on education and real estate using foreign earnings.

The increasing power of digital media and education reforms has also spurred social change in Barnala. Nevertheless, caste-based disparities, gender inequalities, and rural-urban divides remain. *Dalits*, comprising much of the farming community as wage labourers, remain underdeveloped on dimensions of land, education, and social advancement. Efforts from the government regarding decentralized planning, rural development, and positive actions have been efforts to bring parity to this reality, yet still there is a lacuna at the implementation and grassroots effects levels (Planning Commission of India, 2013). Overall, Barnala is a district in which the collision of historical heritage, cultural depth, and unfolding socio-economic changes is alive and well. Its agricultural base, robust Sikh identity, and developing industrial economy provide the context for a society that is slowly coming to terms with the imperatives of modernization and struggling to deal with deep-seated social ills. Attempts to bridge gender and caste divides, enhance education, and create inclusive development are essential if Barnala's future is to be defined.

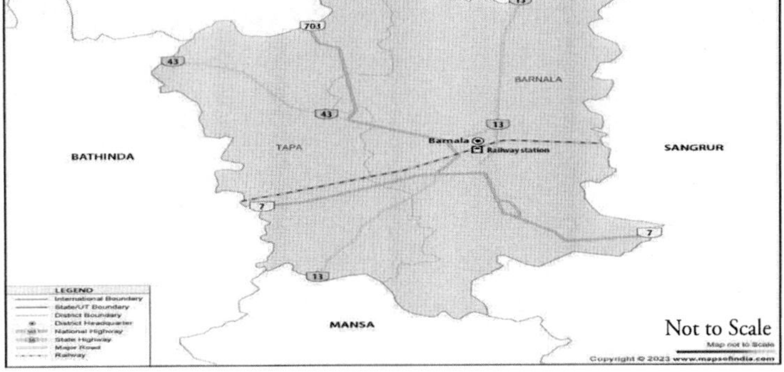

Fig. 3.3

Source: https://www.mapsofindia.com/maps/punjab/districts/barnala.htm

Jalandhar

Jalandhar, which is in north-western Punjab, is one of the most historic and current eminent districts in the state. Physically, Jalandhar lies in the productive Doaba valley, between the Beas and Sutlej rivers. Its position has gifted it with bountiful alluvial soil, making it one of the most fertile farming regions in the state. The fertile plains have been traditionally home to a variety of crops like wheat, rice, and sugarcane, which have been a major contributor to the agrarian economy of Punjab (Government of Punjab, n.d.; Census 2011). Its convenient position with accessibility through major highways and rail networks has also facilitated urbanization and industrialization, making it a major urban centre of northern India.

In the past, Jalandhar has seen a chain of political changes and has served as a key administrative and military hub for successive empires. In the early 16th century, it was awarded as a jagir to Daulat Khan Lodi by Babur in 1524, which indicates its political and strategic significance during the Mughal conquest of India. Later, the city became the province of Sher Shah Suri at the time of the emergence of the Sur Empire and was again captured by the Mughals. The region was invaded by Nadir Shah of Persia at the mid-18th century and was also caught in the power struggles between the Marathas and Afghans. With the fall of Mughal rule, Jalandhar finally came under the Sikh Empire with Maharaja Ranjit Singh in the early 19th century. It subsequently fell under British rule following the Anglo-Sikh wars and was a major cantonment town under the British Raj (Wikipedia, 2024; Punjab Government Gazetteers, 2008).

Sociologically, Jalandhar is one of the most cosmopolitan and industrialized districts of Punjab. According to the 2011 Census, its population was over 2.1 million, and it had a fairly balanced sex ratio as well as a literacy rate of about 82.3 percent, which is much higher than the state average. The city population accounts for over half the district, demonstrating a high rate of urbanization and economic diversification. Jalandhar city is globally known for its sports goods industry that manufactures most of India's exported sporting goods. The sector has contributed significantly to the socio-economic development of the district by offering jobs to thousands and bringing about small and medium-scale entrepreneurship (Census 2011, Government of India; District Industrial Profile, Ministry of MSME, 2020).

Culturally, Jalandhar is known for its diversity, modernity, and deeply entrenched customs. Its religious composition, with a Sikh majority followed by Hindus, Christians, and Muslims, promotes a culture of pluralism and communal concord and cultural blending. The district also hosts some of the key educational establishments, media outlets, and entertainment centres in Punjab, establishing it as the seat of cultural production in the province. Specifically, it has yielded numerous famous personalities from the fields of journalism, sports, and performing arts, giving it a broader cultural impact throughout the state and diaspora communities.

Jalandhar also has a high Non-Resident Indian (NRI) concentration, particularly in the Doaba belt. Numerous families have members settled abroad in nations like the UK, Canada, and the USA. This diaspora link has had a far-reaching effect on local society by way of remittances, cultural exchange, and transnational social practices. One tangible consequence is the development of high-end housing colonies, international-standard schools, and charitable donations in healthcare and education areas. This has also been one of the drivers of social problems like altering family structures, generational conflict, and increasing aspiration-driven consumer culture (Planning Commission of India, 2013).

Economically, Jalandhar's diversified profile covering agriculture, industry, services, and international remittances—distinguishes it from more agricultural districts such as Bathinda and Barnala. Its industrial clusters range beyond sports goods to hand tools, leather goods, and auto components. The city is also emerging as an information technology and service hub, with various start-ups and IT parks in recent years.

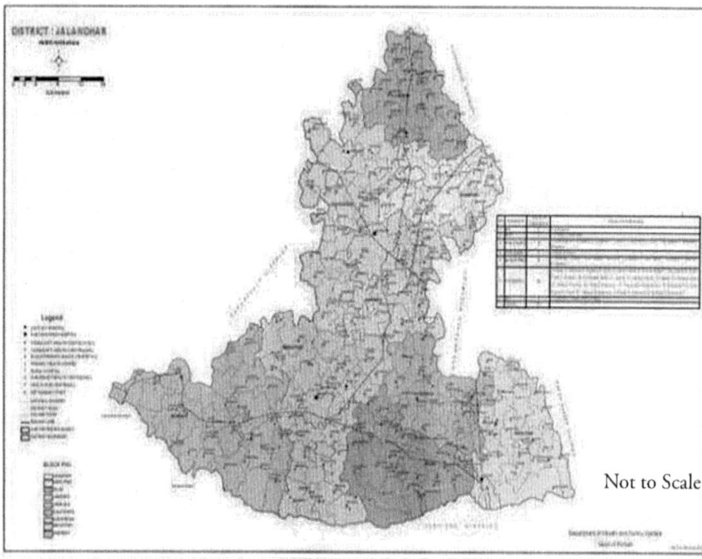

Fig. 3.4

Source: https://www.scribd.com/document/478892493/Jalandhar-City-Map

Punjabi Diaspora : A Historical Context and Sociological Overview

Punjabi diaspora is among the most globalized transnational populations with a history of migrations, socio-economic changes, and political turbulence. Historically, Punjabi migration started with the colonial period as British imperialism enabled mass labour mobility to Southeast Asia, East Africa, and North America. The division of India in 1947 and the Green

Revolution during the 1960s added to migration, especially to the United Kingdom, Canada, and the United States (Government of India, 2022). Presently, Punjabi migrants have made sizeable settlements globally, with Canada having nearly 9,50,000 Punjabis, which constitute one of the largest South Asian ethnic communities. The United Kingdom has approximately 7,50,000 Punjabis, with most being located in urban centres such as London, Birmingham, and Leicester (UK Census Report, 2021). There are about 7,00,000 Punjabi-origin people in the United States, mostly found in California, where farm work and business activities have thrived (US Census Bureau, 2020). Australia has experienced a flood of Punjabi migration, and an estimated 2,50,000 people make Punjabi one of Australia's most rapidly growing languages (Australian Bureau of Statistics, 2021). Malaysia and Singapore together contain more than 1,50,000 Punjabis in Southeast Asia, who are mainly descendants of migrants from colonial times (Government of Malaysia, 2019). The Middle East region, specifically Saudi Arabia and the UAE, boasts close to 1.2 million Punjabi migrant labourers working in the construction and services industries (Government of Punjab, 2023). This presence has far-reaching sociological ramifications, affecting cultural integration, economic remittances, and negotiations of identity within host societies. Punjabi migrants also sustain close attachment to their home country via remittances, cultural exchange, and political identities and affiliations, exhibiting a twin sense of belonging that testifies to both globalization and history.

Research Design

The current study takes a qualitative research methodology to explore the socio-cultural and historical contributions of the Punjabi diaspora to nation-building. The study utilizes a multi-method research strategy, blending historical analysis, ethnographic investigation, and narrative inquiry to develop an exhaustive understanding of the diaspora's creative processes. The investigation explores the dynamic interaction between transnational migration, cultural production, and socio-political engagement by Punjabi migrants during various historical periods. The qualitative method provides the opportunity for a rich investigation of lived experiences, shared memories, and developing diasporic identities.

Data Collection Methods

A. Historical Analysis

The research performs a rigorous historical analysis through the investigation of archival documents, government reports, and historical literature on the migration trends and contributions of the Punjabi diaspora. The analysis is concentrated on major historical periods:

Colonial migrations (19th-20th centuries): Investigating indentured labour and initial trade networks that constructed Punjabi settlements overseas.

Post-independence migration waves (1947–present): Examining the impact of political and economic changes in India and host nations on migration patterns.

Diasporic activism and nation-building initiatives: Examining the contribution of Punjabi expatriates to independence struggles, economic development of Punjab, and political participation in host countries.

B. Ethnographic Research and Narrative Inquiry

Using ethnographic practices such as participant observation and in-depth interviews, personal stories and lived experiences are documented. Engaging with the Punjabi migrants, community figures, and culture practitioners in varying global sites, the research encompasses individual and group memories, the experience of migration, cultural process of adaptation, and attempts to maintaining Punjabi heritage while forging their host society.

C. Case Studies

Case studies are chosen to show the influence of particular individuals, organizations, and movements in the diaspora. These are: Punjabi authors, film-makers, and musicians who work towards the promotion and global dissemination of Punjabi culture. For this project we also used 4 case studies responded for this study of which 3 from Canada, 1 from USA and 1 from Australia.

D. Digital and Media Analysis

The research integrates digital ethnography through the examination of online sites that constitute Punjabi identity and transnational participation. These include:

- Social media sites (YouTube, Instagram, Facebook, diaspora websites) as sites of cultural expression and mobilization of communities.
- Diasporic film, literature, and music that capture changing Punjabi identities, hybrid cultural formations, and political debates within the global Punjabi community.
- Online archives and news websites chronicling the historical and contemporary diaspora contributions.

Through these qualitative research techniques, the research offers a multifaceted interpretation of how the Punjabi diaspora manages cultural identity, creates transnational connections, and contributes to nation-building through creative and socio-economic endeavors.

Sampling Strategy

Purposive sampling is used to sample important participants who belong to a variety of professional backgrounds such as scholars, artists, activists, entrepreneurs, and community leaders. There are 25 respondents under study to cover different diaspora regions. The distribution includes 6 participants from Canada, 5 from the Australia, 5 from the UK, 5 from US, and 4 from Italy. This heterogeneous sample allows for comparative analysis and adds depth to the study with several viewpoints on the Punjabi diaspora's creative contributions to nation-building.

Through the integration of these qualitative research approaches, the study offers a rich understanding of how the Punjabi diaspora negotiates cultural identity, builds transnational connections, and makes creative and socio-economic contributions to nation-building.

Data Analysis Techniques

A. Thematic Analysis

Thematic analysis is used in the study to determine common themes and patterns in interviews, literature, and media content on creative and nation-building activities.

B. Discourse Analysis

A discourse analysis method analyzes how the Punjabi diaspora frames narratives of identity, belonging, and their contribution to nation-building.

C. Comparative Analysis

Comparative analysis is carried out to analyze differences in political and socio-cultural participation across different Punjabi diaspora groups. This enables an understanding of the variability of their contribution and the determinants of their participation.

Ethical Considerations

Ethical guidelines are rigorously followed in this research. Informed consent is taken from all the interviewees, assuring voluntary cooperation. Confidentiality and anonymity are ensured where they are sought, and cultural and political sensitivities to the involvement of the Punjabi diaspora in homeland politics are carefully heeded.

Limitations of the Study

The research also recognizes some of the limitations such as limited access to historical information and participants. Also, self-reported accounts could bring potential biases in the determination of diasporic contributions. Geographical factors also limit broad coverage of all the large-scale diaspora groups. Notwithstanding these challenges, the research applies stringent qualitative methodologies to provide reliability and depth in analysis.

4

Data Analysis

Data Analysis

Section 1: Demographic Information

1. Age Group:

- 18-25
- 26-35
- 36-45
- 46-55
- 56+

The demographic distribution of the diaspora from Bathinda, Barnala, and Jalandhar, residing in Canada, the US, Australia, the UK, and Italy, shows varied age groups. The majority, 8 individuals (32%), fall within the 18-25 age group, followed by 6 (24%) in the 26-35 category. The 36-45 age group comprises 5 individuals (20%), while 3 (12%) are in the 46-55 range. Another 3 (12%) are aged 56 and above. The data

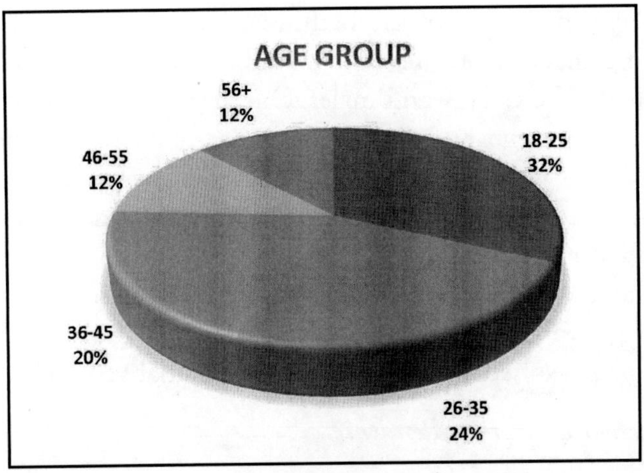

Fig. 4.1

indicates a strong presence of younger generations among the diaspora, reflecting migration trends and generational shifts within these overseas Punjabi communities.

2. Gender

- Male
- Female.

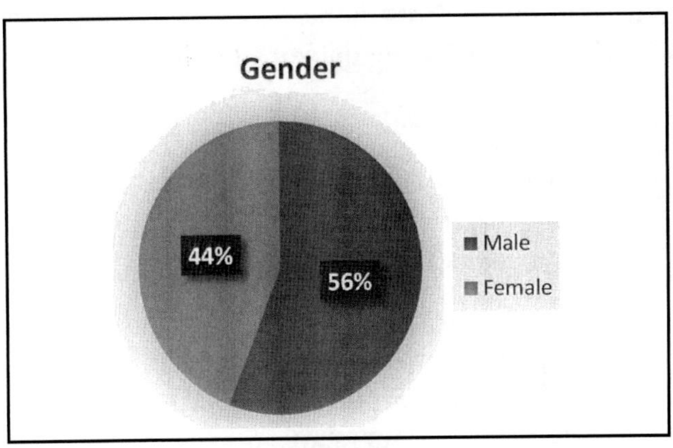

Fig. 4.2

The gender split of the Bathinda, Barnala, and Jalandhar diaspora in Canada, the US, Australia, the UK, and Italy is marginally skewed towards males. Out of the total respondents, 14 (56%) are males and 11 (44%) are females. The split indicates a fairly equal gender split, albeit with more males. The pattern can be interpreted as possibly resulting from trends in migration due to work opportunities, family reunions, or personal ambitions. The fact that there is a large number of females also indicates a growing involvement of women in migration, education, and the professional sphere within these overseas Punjabi communities.

3. Current Country of Residence

The present nation of residence among the Bathinda, Barnala, and Jalandhar diaspora is spread over five countries. Canada has the largest number, with 6 people (24%). Australia, the UK, and the US each have 5 people (20%). In contrast, 4 people (16%) live in Italy. This pattern suggests a high preference for migration to English-speaking nations, most probably due to economic prospects, educational opportunities, and settled Punjabi communities. Italy's appearance in the statistics indicates the increased attractiveness of Europe as a region for migration. The distribution of respondents in these countries captures varying patterns of migration among the Punjabi diaspora.

4. Generational Status in Diaspora:

- First-generation migrant
- Second-generation
- Third-generation or beyond.

The diaspora of Bathinda, Barnala, and Jalandhar settled in Canada, the US, Australia, the UK, and Italy has a diverse generational composition. 9 (36%) are first-generation migrants, which represents new patterns of migration. 6 (24%) are second-generation migrants, i.e., migrant parents have given birth to

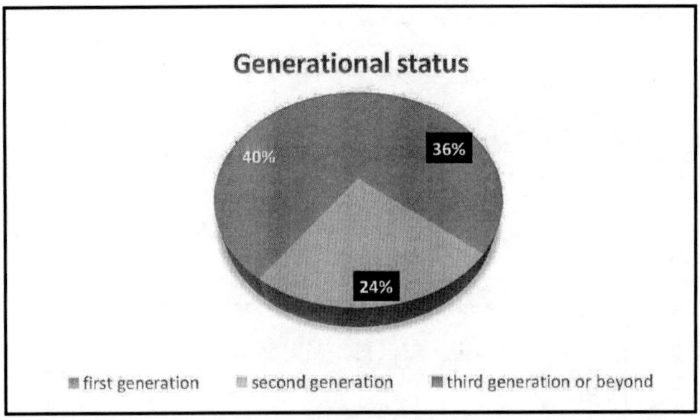

Fig. 4.3

them. 10 (40%) are third-generation or more, reflecting long-standing Punjabi diaspora communities overseas. The presence of several generations indicates long-term settlement, cultural adaptation, and the continuation of Punjabi heritage across various nations while blending into various social and economic environments.

5. Occupation

Diverse professional routes are reflected in the occupational distribution of the diaspora from Bathinda, Barnala, and Jalandhar in Canada, the US, Australia, the UK, and Italy. Many people work in skilled fields including information technology, engineering, and healthcare. Others support local economies by working in retail, business, and entrepreneurship. A significant number are employed in the manufacturing, construction, and transportation sectors. While some responders work in government or administrative capacities, others are students pursuing higher education. Both upward mobility and the persistence of conventional employment trends among the Punjabi diaspora in various nations are highlighted by this distribution.

Section 2: Socio-cultural Influence & Identity

6. How strongly do you identify with Punjabi culture?

- Very strongly
- Moderately
- Slightly
- Not at all.

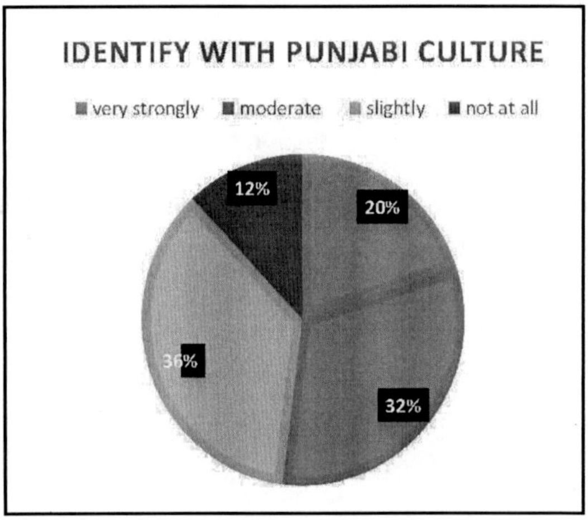

Fig. 4.4

Individuals in the diaspora from Bathinda, Barnala, and Jalandhar who live in Canada, the US, Australia, the UK, and Italy have differing degrees of affiliation with Punjabi culture. Eight respondents (32%) identify with their Punjabi heritage in a moderate way, whilst five respondents (20%) feel a very strong connection to it. There is a shift in cultural affiliation over generations, as evidenced by the largest group of responders, 9 (36%), who feel only a modest connection. Three people (12%), on the other hand, do not identify with Punjabi culture at all, indicating complete assimilation into their host nations. This pattern demonstrates differing levels of cultural adaption and retention.

7. Do you think the Punjabi diaspora helps preserve Punjab's cultural heritage?

- Yes, significantly
- To some extent
- No effect
- It dilutes Punjabi culture.

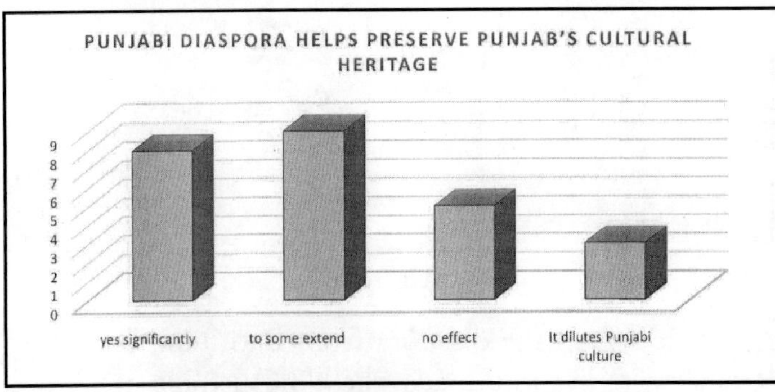

Fig. 4.5

People from Bathinda, Barnala, and Jalandhar who live in Canada, the US, Australia, the UK, and Italy have differing opinions about the contribution of the Punjabi diaspora to the preservation of Punjab's cultural legacy. Eight respondents (32%) think that the diaspora plays a major role in maintaining Punjabi culture through language, customs, and social gatherings. Nine more people (36%) believe it helps to some degree. Five respondents (20%), however, believe that the diaspora has little impact, maybe as a result of generations of cultural dilution. Furthermore, three people (12%) think that migration erodes Punjabi cultural identity, which reflects worries about assimilation and shifting customs overseas.

8. How often do you participate in Punjabi cultural events (festivals, music, dance)?

- Regularly

- Occasionally
- Rarely
- Never.

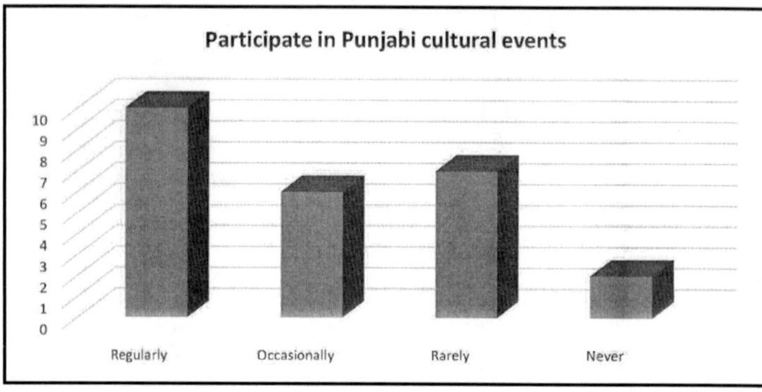

Fig. 4.6

Individuals in the diaspora from Bathinda, Barnala, and Jalandhar who live in Canada, the US, Australia, the UK, and Italy vary in their involvement in Punjabi cultural events. Ten respondents (40%) said they regularly take part in dancing, music, and festivals, demonstrating a high level of cultural participation. Six more people (24%) attend sporadically, indicating a moderate level of connection. In the meantime, 7 responders (28%) hardly ever participate, which over time indicates a deteriorating cultural connection. Furthermore, two people (8%) never participate in such activities, indicating total disengagement. Different levels of cultural involvement are highlighted by this distribution, which is impacted by absorption into host societies and generational disparities.

9. Should Punjabi language education be promoted more in diaspora communities?

- Strongly agree
- Agree
- Neutral
- Disagree.

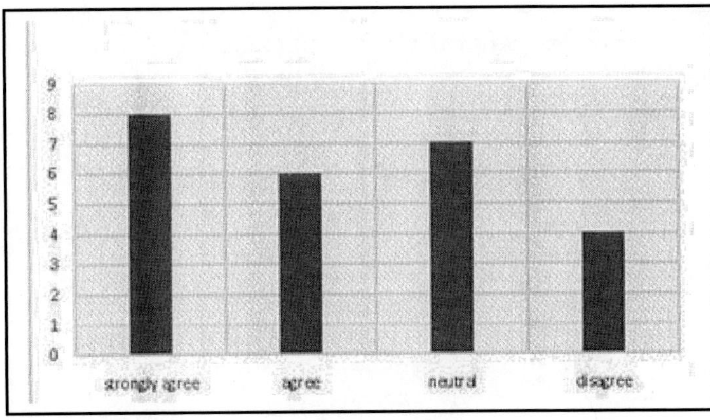

Fig. 4.7

People from Bathinda, Barnala, and Jalandhar who live in Canada, the US, Australia, the UK, and Italy have differing opinions about the importance of advancing Punjabi language education in diaspora communities. According to 8 respondents (32%) who emphasised the value of language in maintaining cultural identity, Punjabi education should be promoted. Six more people (24%) concur, indicating a favourable propensity for language retention. Seven replies, or 28 percent, are ambivalent, expressing hesitancy or lack of interest. Furthermore, 4 people (16%) disagree, citing issues like integration, a lack of resources, or Punjabi's diminished significance in diaspora groups' day-to-day lives.

10. Do younger generations in the diaspora maintain Punjabi traditions as much as older generations?

- Yes, even more
- About the same
- Less than older generations
- Almost no connection.

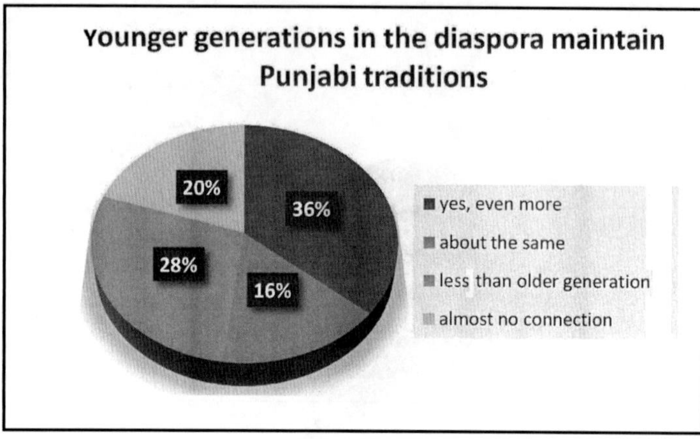

Fig. 4.8

The degree to which younger diasporic generations uphold Punjabi customs in comparison to their elder counterparts differs among Bathinda, Barnala, and Jalandhar people living in Canada, the United States, Australia, the United Kingdom, and Italy. Possibly as a result of cultural pride and concerted community efforts, nine respondents (36%) think younger generations continue to respect customs even more. In the meantime, four people (16%) believe they uphold traditions to a comparable degree. Cultural assimilation and generational changes in identity are evident, though, as five respondents (20%) see virtually no relationship and seven respondents (28%) believe younger generations participate less in cultural customs.

Section 3: Economic Contributions & Transnational Networks

11. Do you or your family send remittances (money) to Punjab?

- Yes, regularly
- Occasionally
- No.

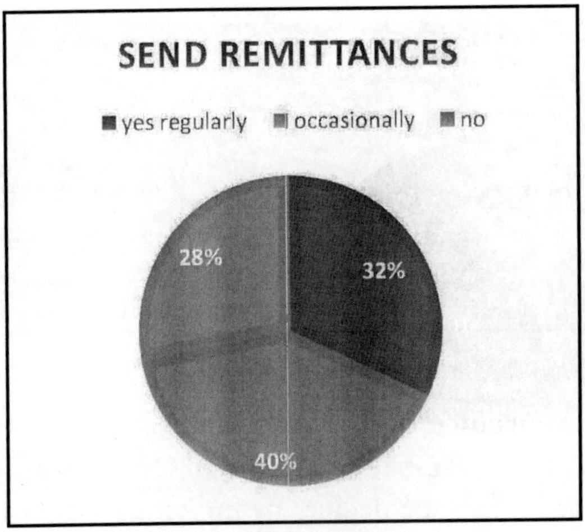

Fig. 4.9

The remittances sent to Punjab by Bathinda, Barnala and Jalandhar natives living in Canada, the US, Australia, the UK and Italy are different. In total, 8 respondents (32%) regularly send money, to family members, businesses or investments in their hometowns. Another 10 individuals (40%) remit occasionally; most likely on special occasions or during emergencies. On the other hand, 7 respondents (28%) do not send remittances as financial connections between the diaspora and Punjab while also reflecting migration patterns and family relocation their immediate families already live with them in their host countries. This distribution highlights the ongoing but uneven economic ties between the Punjabi diaspora and their places of origin, shaped by migration trajectories and family settlement patterns.

12. How important are diaspora investments (NRI real estate, businesses) for Punjab's economy?

- Very important
- Somewhat important
- Not important.

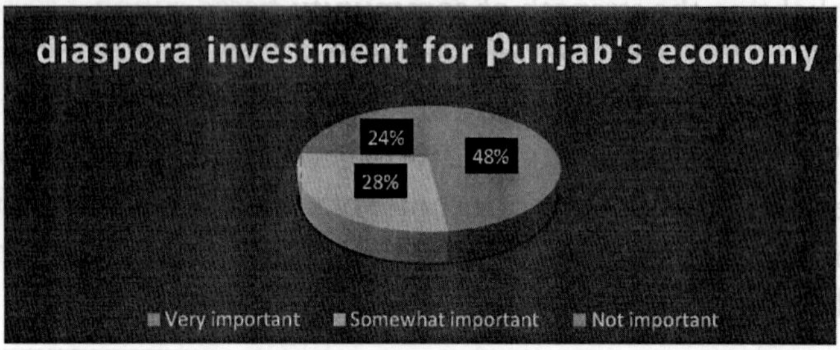

Fig. 4.10

The importance of diaspora investments such as NRI contributions to real estate and businesses for Punjab's economy is recognized to varying degrees by individuals from Bathinda, Barnala, and Jalandhar residing in Canada, the US, Australia, the UK, and Italy. A majority of 12 respondents (48%) consider such investments very important, highlighting their role in boosting local development and infrastructure. Another 7 individuals (28%) view them as somewhat important, acknowledging their impact but possibly with some reservations. Meanwhile, 6 respondents (24%) believe these investments are not important, suggesting scepticism about their long-term benefits or concerns over rising property prices and displacement.

13. Have you or someone you know benefited from job/business networks linked to Punjab?

- Yes
- No.

Job and business networks linked to Punjab have played a significant role in supporting the diaspora from Bathinda, Barnala, and Jalandhar residing in Canada, the US, Australia, the UK, and Italy. A total of 17 respondents (68%) stated that they or someone they know have benefited from such networks, highlighting the strength of community-based support systems that facilitate employment, entrepreneurship, and smoother settlement in foreign countries. In contrast, 8 respondents (32%) expressed no such advantage, indicating either poor access to these networks or a choice of independent routes. This information highlights the importance of Punjabi social capital in diaspora success stories.

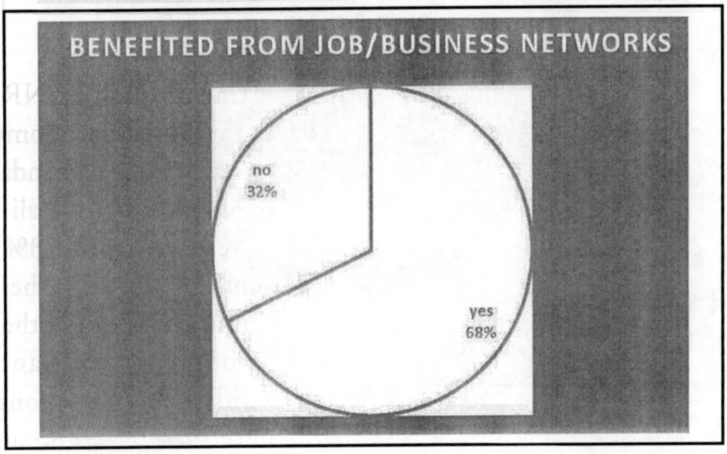

Fig. 4.11

14. Do you believe Punjab's government effectively utilizes diaspora contributions for development?

- Yes, very effectively
- Somewhat effectively
- Not effectively.

Perceptions of the degree to which Punjab's government uses diaspora remittances to implement development differ among the Bathinda, Barnala, and Jalandhar residing in Canada, the US, Australia, the UK, and Italy. 12 respondents (48%) hold the view that the government employs these remittances very effectively with visible effects on infrastructure, education, and welfare within the community. Another 9 respondents (36%) think the government is sort of effective, perhaps highlighting inefficiency or insufficient transparency. While 4 respondents (16%) think the contributions are not effectively used, which reflects worries about mismanagement or insufficient communication between the state and the diaspora.

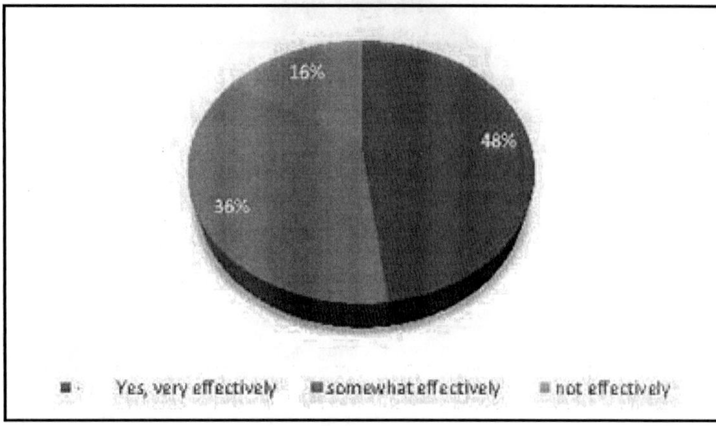

Fig. 4.12

Section 4: Political Influence & Governance

15. Should the Punjabi diaspora have voting rights in Punjab's elections?

- Yes
- No.

Views regarding giving voting rights to the Punjabi diaspora in Punjab's polls are clearly split among Bathinda, Barnala, and Jalandhar based in Canada, the US, Australia, Britain, and Italy. 9 respondents (36%) believe the diaspora deserves voting rights, perhaps an expression of their emotional and economic interests remaining linked with Punjab. But 16 (64%) are against the notion, pointing out that those who have gained foreign citizenship or lost Indian citizenship are legally disqualified to vote. This view stresses the significance of residency and national loyalty in defining political engagement.

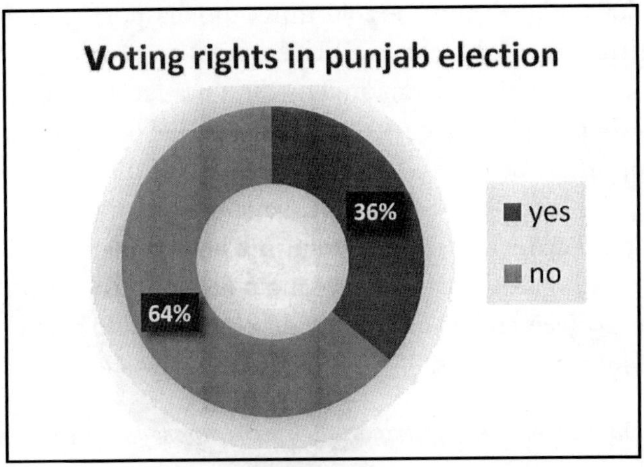

Fig. 4.13

16. How influential is the diaspora in shaping Punjab's political policies?

- Very influential
- Somewhat influential
- Not influential.

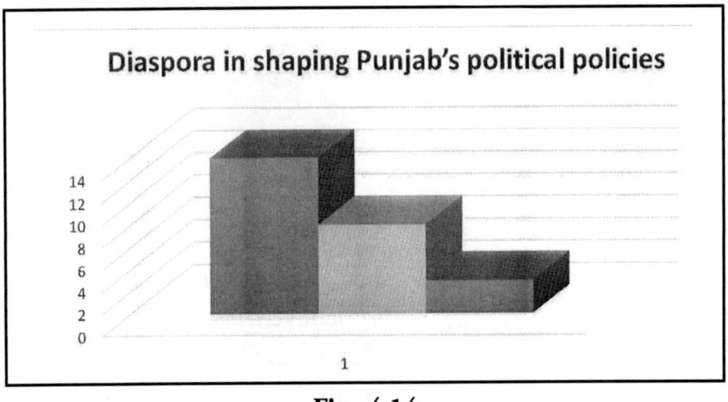

Fig. 4.14

Punjab's political views are thought to be significantly influenced by the Punjabi diaspora from Bathinda, Barnala, and Jalandhar, who now live in Canada, the US, Australia, the UK, and Italy. Eight people (32%) think the diaspora is somewhat significant, whilst the majority of 14 respondents (56%) think it is highly influential. The diaspora has little influence, according to just three respondents (12%). Their participation is important because of their investments, cultural advocacy, financial transfers, and unofficial political lobbying, even though they have few voting rights. They have a greater say in determining regional objectives and policy directions because of their involvement in community development and relationships with local authorities.

17. Do diaspora-led protests or advocacy impact governance reforms in Punjab?

- Yes, significantly
- Somewhat
- No effect.

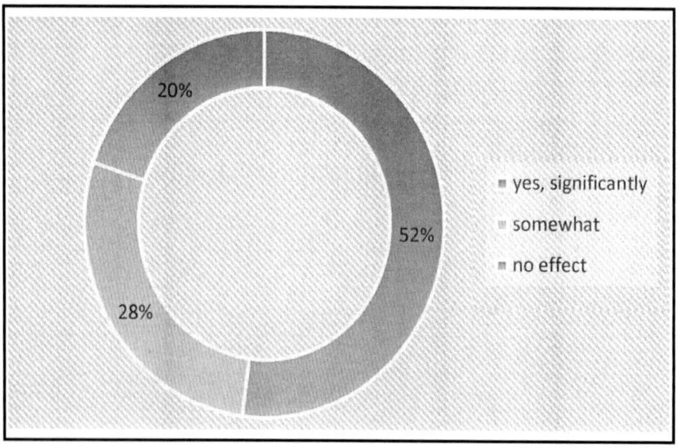

Fig. 4.15

Individuals from Bathinda, Barnala, and Jalandhar who live in Canada, the US, Australia, the UK, and Italy believe that campaigning and protests led by the diaspora have a significant impact on governance improvements in Punjab. Thirteen respondents (52%) think that these initiatives have a big influence, especially when it comes to defining agendas, putting pressure on other countries, and raising money. Seven more people (28%) believe they have some influence, depending on the problem and Punjab's political situation. Five respondents (20%), however, saw no impact, most likely as a result of the lack of immediate structural improvements. The information demonstrates the increasing influence of the diaspora on Punjab's socio-political scene.

18. Which area should the diaspora focus on most for Punjab's development?

- Education & Healthcare
- Agricultural Modernization
- Industrial & Job Growth
- Cultural Preservation.

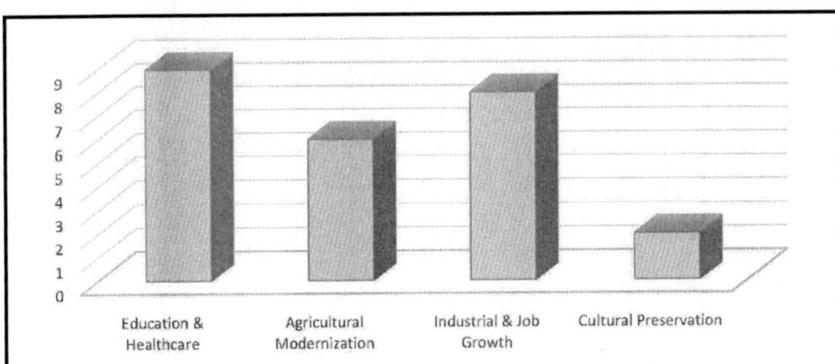

Fig. 4.16

Respondents from Bathinda, Barnala, and Jalandhar living in Canada, the US, Australia, the UK, and Italy gave a range of answers when asked which region the diaspora should focus on for Punjab's growth. Nine respondents (36%) prioritised healthcare and education, indicating a desire to enhance access to necessary services and quality of life. Eight people (32%) cited industrial and job growth, referring to economic advancement and work prospects. Six respondents (24%) supported agricultural modernization, highlighting the continued importance of the sector. Only two people (8%) gave cultural preservation top priority, indicating that other developmental requirements come first.

Section 5: Transnational Identity & Future Engagement

19. Do you feel more connected to Punjab or your country of residence?

- Strongly connected to Punjab
- Balanced connection to both
- More connected to country of residence
- Fully assimilated abroad.

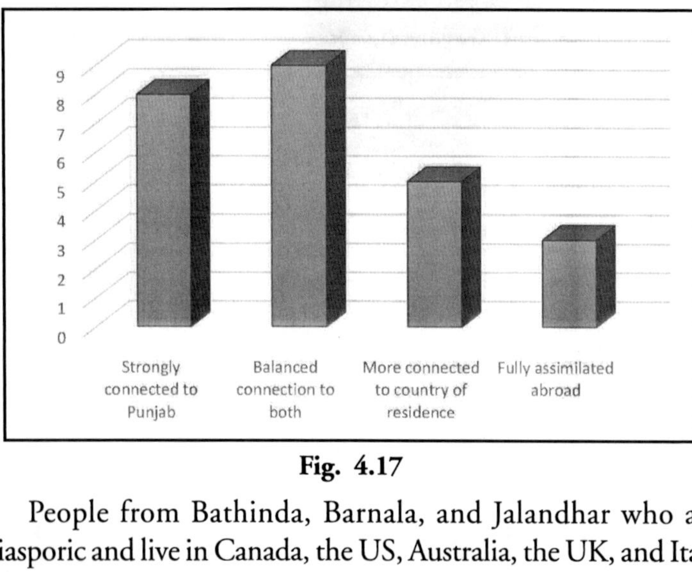

Fig. 4.17

People from Bathinda, Barnala, and Jalandhar who are diasporic and live in Canada, the US, Australia, the UK, and Italy have different feelings about Punjab and their home country. Eight respondents (32%) had a strong sense of emotional and cultural ties to Punjab. A balanced connection to both locations is reported by nine more people (36%) indicating dual identity and active participation in both societies. In contrast, three respondents (12%) have fully assimilated overseas, while five respondents (20%) feel more linked to their home country, demonstrating generational transitions and greater cultural integration.

20. Would you consider returning to Punjab permanently if opportunities improved?

- Yes
- No
- Maybe.

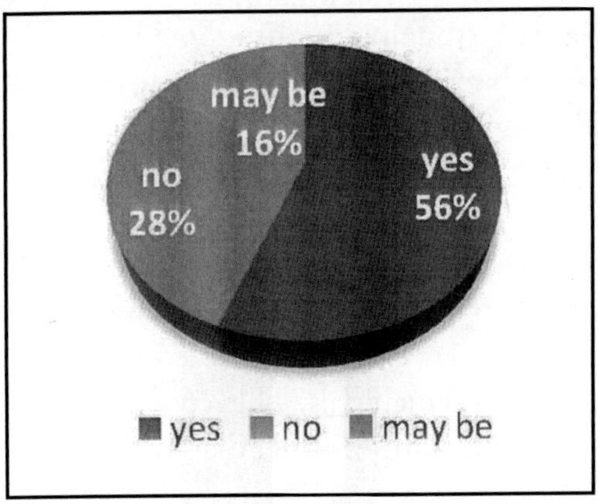

Fig. 4.18

Many respondents from Bathinda, Barnala, and Jalandhar who now live in Canada, the US, Australia, the UK, and Italy said they would be eager to move back to Punjab permanently if there were better possibilities. 14 respondents (56%) said "yes", frequently claiming a preference for cultural origins, a desire to contribute to their nation, or personal attachment.

Seven more respondents (28%) responded "no", most likely because they had solid jobs, families, or lifestyles overseas. Four people (16%), on the other hand, gave the "maybe" response, indicating conditional interest depending on variables including jobs, infrastructure, and governance. These opinions point to the possibility of reverse migration in the event that circumstances improve.

Case Study Analysis (Case from Ethnographic Studies)

Case Study 1: Cultural Affiliation and Digital Identity (Canada)

Respondent: (25, University Student, Toronto, Canada)

The respondent, who is a second-generation immigrant from North India, is a student studying Sociology. They actively participate in online communities focusing on K-pop, Chinese dramas, and Japanese anime.

Case Narrative

The respondent's initiation into East Asian digital content commenced in high school. Social networking sites such as TikTok, Instagram, and Reddit enabled exposure to Korean and Chinese cultural materials. They aver that they find more affinity toward these cultures rather than their native indigenous origins. Their interactions among fans, with many of which were in the English language while using some Korean terms, have dominated their level of proficiency within their native tribal language.

Analysis

- Digital proximity has transformed cultural identity among new generations.

- Choice of overseas media reconfigures language patterns, resulting in reduced native language maintenance.
- Online social ties create a sense of belonging, which substitutes for heritage cultural affiliations.

Conclusion

This example illustrates how online sites reconfigure cultural identities and language tastes. The growing prevalence of East Asian media among North Indian diasporic youth points to the importance of proactive measures for cultural preservation.

Case Study 2: Social Media and Shifting Linguistic Trends (Canada)

Respondent: (30, IT Professional, Vancouver, Canada)

The respondent, hailing from North India, migrated to Canada ten years ago. He is multilingual, conversant in English, Hindi, and his native language, but says he uses his indigenous language less often.

Case Narrative

The respondent connects his decreasing fluency in their language with extensive use of English in official and social arenas. English is used as the dominant form of communication with their colleagues and friends. Algorithms used by social media platforms have continued to increase exposure to English and Korean pop culture at the expense of indigenous language content. Whenever they go home to their hometown, they can barely communicate using their mother tongue.

Analysis

- Social media perpetuates the prevailing linguistic trends, resulting in cultural and linguistic attrition.

- **Migrants are subject to double pressure:** Occupational adjustment and cultural maintenance.
- The function of new media in transforming language use should attract more academic attention.

Conclusion

This example demonstrates how social media and workplaces speed up linguistic change. This is a cause for concern regarding the viability of local languages within migrant groups.

Case Study 3: Korean Wave and Youth Identity (USA)

Respondent: (22, Fashion Student, New York, USA)

The respondent, belonging to North Indian community has been a passionate fan of K-pop and Korean fashion since the age of 15.

Case Narrative

The interest of the respondent in Korean culture started with K-dramas. Eventually, they adopted Korean fashion and even incorporated Hangul (Korean script) into their virtual life. They engage with other K-culture fans, establishing virtual friendships that have substituted traditional community interactions. They complain about the absence of contemporary representation of their own culture in mainstream media, which they feel is leading to its unpopularity among younger generations.

Analysis

- Aesthetic and cyber influences redefine cultural aspirations.
- The absence of local media representation promotes cultural movement towards foreign trends.

- Cultural battlegrounds are the online platforms, in which global and local influences clash.

Conclusion

This case emphasizes the importance of indigenous content development as a counter to cultural dilution. It also underscores the potent influence of aesthetics on youth identity.

Case Study 4: Cultural Hybridization Among Indigenous Youth (Australia)

Respondent: (28, Marketing Professional, Sydney, Australia)

The respondent was brought up in a North Indian community and migrated to Australia later. They consider themselves a "global citizen" and report mixed cultural influences.

Case Narrative

The respondent watches a blend of Western, Korean, and Indian programming. Their identity is an internal part of their heritage but only infrequently outwardly expressed. They socialize with peers who share their online and pop-culture interests, and it becomes hard to identify with their native community at home. Their parents promote cultural maintenance, but they struggle to span the generation gap.

Analysis

- Migration and digital globalization produce hybrid identities.
- The gap in cultural preservation over generations is expanding.
- Hybridity can be a factor for cultural erosion if deliberate efforts for preservation are not taken.

Conclusion

The issue here identifies the intricacies of hybrid identity in migrant youths. Indigenous cultures risk further alienation without deliberate intervention.

Overall Analysis

These case studies illustrate that digital globalization, migration, and social media have a significant influence on cultural identity and language retention among North Indian youth. The challenge lies in maintaining modern influences and traditional roots.

Case Study Analysis (Secondary Data)

Introduction

The Punjabi diaspora has been a key player in the international spread and promotion of Punjabi culture in its many forms, such as literature, drama, and music. The movement of Punjabis to far-flung regions around the world, notably North America and Europe, has given rise to a vibrant and diverse diasporic identity that remains dynamic in nature yet firmly rooted in its cultural heritage. This essay explores the work of two prominent figures of the Punjabi diaspora: Ajmer Rode, a Canadian playwright and writer, and Anita Lerche, a Danish-born singer who has immersed herself in Punjabi music. In a close-up sociological focus, this research investigates their role in Punjabi cultural representation and the transnational forces that have influenced their work.

Ajmer Rode: A Literary Light in the Punjabi Diaspora

Ajmer Rode's writings have played a key role in establishing a cultural link between the diaspora and the Punjabi homeland.

His works include poetry, drama, prose, and translation, indicating the multifaceted nature of diasporic identity and cultural shifts that the Punjabis in Canada underwent.

Contributions to Literature

Rode's initial forays into writing came in the form of *Vishava Di Nuhār* (1966), released by Punjabi University, which approached Einstein's Theory of Relativity via fictional discussion. This project saw Rode begin his own forays into intellectual and scientific thought within Punjabi literature. His most distinguished work of poetry, *Leela*, written collaboratively with Navtej Bharati, is an expansive 1,200-page volume that was celebrated for the experimental nature with which it has approached poetic exploration.

In recognition by the Anād Foundation in Delhi, *Leela* received the 2011 poetry award for its singular exploration of poetic language, cultural memory, and existential struggle. Rode's poetry frequently intersects with themes of displacement, migration, and socio-political reality of the Punjabi diaspora. His writing is highly reflective, combining individual experiences with more general social and political narratives reflecting the struggles of immigrant communities.

Contributions to Theatre

Rode is also credited with establishing Canadian Punjabi drama. His play *Komagata Maru* was among the first complete-length Punjabi plays performed in Canada, which celebrated the historical 1914 Komagata Maru case, in which a vessel of South Asian immigrants was refused entry into Canada based on racist immigration laws. This play is both a historical account and a commentary on exclusionary policies that have determined diasporic conditions.

Rode's *Rebirth of Gandhi*, a British play performed at the Surrey Arts Center in 2004, also illustrates his interest in cross-cultural themes. Through this play, Rode examines the applicability of Gandhian thought to modern-day global conflicts in a dialogue between past and present. His active association with the Punjabi Writers Forum in Vancouver and his stint with the National Council of The Writers Union of Canada attest to his interest in nurturing Punjabi drama and literature in Canada.

Anita Lerche: Bridging Cultures Through Punjabi Music

Anita Lerche, a Danish vocalist, has been at the forefront in making Punjabi music globally popular. Contrary to what is expected of diasporic artists who pass down Punjabi heritage, Lerche's immersion in Punjabi music was by choice, which symbolizes the transcultural popularity of Punjabi artistic works.

Journey into Punjabi Music

Lerche's interest in Punjabi music started while on a 2005 trek in the Indian Himalayas. Her profound love took her to Hoshiarpur, Punjab, where she stayed for three months to study the language and musical culture under the tutelage of local guides. Her rigorous method of learning the subtleties of Punjabi music enabled her to release *Heer* from Denmark in 2006, becoming the first Western woman to do so.

The album contains classic Punjabi songs, and her version of "Heer", drawn from the epic love story *Heer Ranjha* by Waris Shah, has gained extensive popularity. The critics have praised her natural pronunciation, emotional intensity, and capacity to bring out the feeling of Punjabi folk tradition.

Cultural Ambassador and Global Recognition

After her early success, Lerche went on to release Punjabi albums like *Sadke Punjab Ton*, further establishing herself as an international cultural ambassador. Her music, blending classical Punjabi folk sounds with modern flavours, has caught on with both diasporic and non-Punjabi listeners.

Lerche has been the recipient of several awards, most recently the Global Punjabi Society Award for Conspicuous Singer in 2013. Apart from her professional success in music, she has been involved in humanitarian activities as well, partnering with non-profit organizations like Christel House International to support education among needy children in India, Mexico, South Africa, and the United States. Her humanitarian work supports her conviction of the potential of music as an instrument of social transformation and cross-cultural communication.

Data Analysis: Digital and Media Representation of Punjabi Identity

The virtual environment is important in constructing and consolidating Punjabi identity throughout transnational publics. Media websites like YouTube, Instagram, and Facebook are gregarious spaces for the practice of culture that allow diaspora populations to negotiate identity, carry out political debate, and mobilize the collective consciousness. For example, diaspora Punjabi youth are actively engaged in digital storytelling and utilize short-form videos and cultural memes to affirm hybrid identities combining their heritage and their host countries (Gibson, 2020). The spread of diasporic cinema, music, and literature also adds to the identity creation. Punjabi music, especially fusion *Bhangra* and hip-hop, has had strong popularity on streaming sites with artists incorporating multilingual lyrics and cross-cultural imagery, capturing an unstructured diasporic experience (Sandhu, 2019).

Furthermore, online newspapers and news archives offer historical and contemporary accounts detailing the changing function of the Punjabi diaspora in international socio-economic and political affairs. Online spaces such as the Punjab Digital Library and diaspora-led news websites are sites of collectivity of community history, promoting continuity and collective memory (Johal, 2021). The online spaces also provide a platform for advocacy around farm rights movements, immigration policies, and Sikh identity politics and how digital media serves as a link between local and global activism (Kaur & Kalra, 2022). Through qualitative digital ethnography, the following are the findings that show how online activity plays a role in upholding cultural identity, re-enforcing transnational relations, and supporting both the homeland and host countries' economies.

5

Historical Evolution of the Punjabi Diaspora

5.1 Early Migration: Colonial and Post-Colonial Contexts

Early Punjabi migration, especially in the colonial and post-colonial era, needs to be interpreted not merely as the physical movement of people but as a socially entrenched process of socio-historical provenance which developed from and reproduced certain power structures, domination, and resistance. These patterns of migration were not independent, free-willed flows but were shaped by the overarching forces of colonial rule, capitalist expansion, and socio-political dislocation. Under British colonial rule, Punjab was strategically incorporated into the imperial military machinery and economic system. Its agrarian economy was reconfigured to function in colonial extraction, and its inhabitants were incorporated into a regime of discipline, taxation, and militarization. Migration from Punjab under colonial times was therefore both a product of and a reaction to these externally imposed changes.

Colonial policies provided both the push and pull factors that motivated early migration. On the one hand, land revenue systems, commodification of agriculture, and the encouragement of cash crops resulted in small farmers growing more dependent upon market fluctuations and debt, and hence rural distress and displacement. Conversely, overseas opportunities as imperial army soldiers or as plantation and infrastructure workers abroad promised the hope of economic respite and mobility, albeit in exploitative systems. Migration therefore became a survival mechanism within a setting of limited local alternatives and growing global labour needs, directed by colonial regimes of accumulation and control.

The post-colonial era introduced a new level of complication to these patterns of migration. The Partition of India in 1947 was not merely a political phenomenon but a violent break that reshaped the social geography of Punjab. It compelled millions of people to migrate across newly delineated boundaries, usually through acts of unimaginable communal violence and dispossession. The trauma of Partition cannot be separated from the experience of migration; it served as both a cause of forced migration and as a constitutive moment in the diasporic consciousness of Punjabis. Families were displaced, identities were violently remapped along religious lines, and community solidarities were broken or reconstituted in the process of survival and resettlement.

From a sociological point of view, these initial migrations need to be understood in terms of structural inequalities economic, political, and cultural that made some populations more mobile, and others more vulnerable. Migration came to reflect deeply ingrained disparities along lines of caste, class, religion, and gender. For example, upper-caste, landowning Punjabis generally had the means and networks to immigrate overseas or reconstitute their lives in post-Partition India, while lower-caste and landless workers experienced intensified forms of exclusion, frequently being resettled in peripheral urban neighbourhoods or stuck in poverty traps.

Additionally, initial Punjabi migration was also a space of identity negotiation and transformation. Migrants were forced to reconstitute their sense of self, community, and belonging in strange lands, either within India or abroad. This process was influenced both by recollections about the homeland and by the imperative of changing socio-political contexts. Thus, migration served not merely as a demographic or economic phenomenon but as a profoundly cultural and psychological one, with the formation of hybrid identities and transnational connections.

Recruitment of Punjabis as Soldiers and Labourers

The British colonial administration played a pivotal role in shaping the early migration patterns of Punjabis. The Punjab region, known for its agricultural productivity and martial traditions, became a key recruitment ground for the British Indian Army. The British viewed Punjabis, particularly Sikhs, as a "martial race", a colonial construct that essentialized certain ethnic groups as inherently suited for military service (Fox, 1985). This recruitment was not merely a matter of filling army ranks but was deeply tied to the colonial strategy of maintaining control over India. By recruiting Punjabis into the army, the British ensured a loyal force that could suppress dissent within India and serve imperial interests abroad.

The recruitment of Punjabis as soldiers also had significant sociological implications. It created a culture of migration, where military service became a viable livelihood option for many rural Punjabis. This migration was often circular, with soldiers returning to their villages after their service, bringing back not only economic resources but also new ideas and experiences. However, this also reinforced a dependency on colonial structures, as many families relied on remittances from soldiers serving in far-flung parts of the British Empire.

In addition to military recruitment, Punjabis were also mobilized as labourers, particularly in the construction of infrastructure projects such as railways and canals. The colonial economy relied heavily on the exploitation of cheap labour, and Punjabis, often from marginalized communities, were recruited to work in harsh conditions. This labour migration was marked by a lack of agency, as many labourers were driven by economic desperation rather than choice. The sociological impact of this labour migration was profound, as it disrupted traditional agrarian economies and social structures, leading to the proletarianization of many rural Punjabis (Tatla, 1999).

The British colonial government was instrumental in influencing the initial patterns of Punjabi migration. The Punjab province, which was famous for its fertile land and martial culture, emerged as a major recruitment base for the British Indian Army. Punjabis, and especially Sikhs, were considered by the British to be a "martial race", a colonial stereotype that essentialized particular ethnic groups as being naturally predisposed to military service (Fox, 1985). This recruitment was not just a question of filling army ranks but was closely connected to the colonial policy of keeping India under control. By enlisting Punjabis in the army, the British had a loyal force that could quell rebellion within India and advance imperial interests overseas.

The enlistment of Punjabis in the army also had profound sociological consequences. It instilled a culture of migration, where a military career was a feasible livelihood choice for numerous rural Punjabis. Migration was usually circular, with soldiers returning to their villages upon completion of their service, not only carrying economic resources but also novel experiences and ideas. But this also perpetuated a reliance on colonial institutions, since many families depended on money sent back by soldiers stationed in distant reaches of the British Empire.

Apart from military recruitment, Punjabis were also mobilized as workers, mainly for the construction of infrastructure projects like railways and canals. The colonial economy was based on the exploitation of cheap labour, and Punjabis, mostly from poor communities, were mobilized to work in very difficult conditions. The labour migration was characterized by the absence of agency, as the labourers were many times economically desperate and not by choice. The sociological effect of such labour migration was far-reaching since it undermined traditional agrarian societies and economies and resulted in the proletarianization of large numbers of rural Punjabis (Tatla, 1999).

Impact of the Partition of India (1947) on Migration Patterns

The Partition of India in 1947 was a cataclysmic event that reshaped the migration patterns of Punjabis in profound ways. The division of Punjab into Indian and Pakistani territories led to one of the largest forced migrations in human history, with an estimated 14 million people displaced and up to 2 million killed in communal violence (Butalia, 1998). The sociological impact of this migration was immense, as it uprooted entire communities, disrupted social networks, and created a legacy of trauma that continues to affect the Punjabi diaspora.

The Partition migration was marked by a sudden and violent reconfiguration of identities. Punjabis who had coexisted for centuries as neighbours were suddenly divided along religious lines, with Hindus and Sikhs migrating to India and Muslims to Pakistan. This migration was not merely a physical movement but also a psychological and cultural rupture. The trauma of Partition is deeply embedded in the collective memory of the Punjabi diaspora, shaping their sense of identity and belonging (Kaur, 2007).

The post-Partition period also saw a new wave of migration, as many Punjabis sought to escape the economic and social instability caused by the division. This included both rural and urban Punjabis, who migrated to other parts of India or abroad in search of better opportunities. The sociological impact of this migration was complex, as it led to the formation of new diasporic communities while also reinforcing existing inequalities. For example, upper-caste and landowning Punjabis were often better positioned to migrate and establish themselves in new locations, while lower-caste and landless Punjabis faced greater challenges (Judge, 2005).

The socio-cultural break-up resulting from the Partition of India went far beyond physical relocation. The creation of arbitrary borders turned age-old social ties into places of suspicion and hostility. Social groups that had traditionally been held together by common linguistic, regional, and cultural ties were sundered under the burden of communal polarisation. The swift establishment of religious identities as exclusive and oppositional transformed the way Punjabis saw themselves and others, creating an acute identity crisis. This compelled redefinition of community boundaries, where the ethno-religious became the key to categorisation, brought a violent binary that seeped into daily life. Consequently, Punjabi identity, once the paradigm of pluralism, came more and more to be understood in a broken image of "Hindu", "Muslim", or "Sikh", respectively bound to the nation-state and attendant political philosophy.

The sociological term "liminality" is especially handy for describing Punjabis in and after Partition. During this interval of in-betweenness, refugees were placed in a state of suspension neither fully incorporated into their new environments nor cut off from their former places. Refugee camps, transit stations, and resettlement colonies were liminal places where previous social forms were deconstructed and new, tenuous forms of order were forged. These places witnessed a breakdown of the known: caste hierarchies were momentarily disrupted, gender roles were breached, and new solidarities founded on shared pain started emerging. But this solidarity tended to be tenuous, especially in the face of competition for resources, jobs, and state recognition.

Gendered aspects of Partition migration also call for sociological examination. Women not only disproportionately were victimized by abduction, rape, and forced conversion but were also made into symbols of community honour and national identity. The rescue and return of the abducted women by Indian and Pakistani states purported acts of justice frequently took away from these women their agency, reducing them to spoils of war in preference over their status as independent individuals (Butalia, 1998). For most women, Partition trauma was double: the bodily violence they suffered and the social compulsion to be quiet afterwards. Their stories, traditionally marginalized from mainstream histories, demonstrate how the onus of national honour was unfairly placed on women's bodies, and how their silencing ensured patriarchal domination in both migrant and resettled societies.

The reorganization of the Punjabi diaspora following Partition was not an even process. Migration and resettlement were highly stratified by caste, class, and gender. Land-owning Jat Sikhs and Khatris who had means to draw upon kinship and capital networks were frequently able to re-establish themselves relatively rapidly and lucratively, especially in areas such as Delhi, Haryana, and western Uttar Pradesh. Most were granted land or compensation via the newly established schemes of refugee rehabilitation, enabling them to re-establish economic stability and, for some, even increase their agrarian holdings. *Dalits* and landless labourers, on the other hand, were subjected to prolonged marginalisation. Displaced from both labour and land opportunities, many were pushed towards urban informal economies, frequently into low-waged and insecure occupations.

This asymmetry in post-Partition resettlement also determined the spatial geography of migration. While the elite and middle-class Punjabis moved towards urban areas where they could capitalize on education, bureaucratic expertise, or commercial skills, the lower-caste migrants found themselves only in the urban peripheries, refugee colonies, or slums with no access to state favour or political patronage. These new spatial arrangements cemented pre-existing social disparities even as they opened up the possibility of new community formations. Urban refugee colonies, for example, became sites of political mobilization and ethnic solidarity, but also replicated patterns of exclusion and caste segregation within diasporic enclaves.

The emotional aspects of Partition migration loss, longing, and dislocation also influenced the transgenerational identity of the Punjabi diaspora. For most migrants and their children, the memory of a lost homeland became the core of their sense of self. This "nostalgia for roots" was expressed most commonly in oral histories, religious rituals, and cultural celebrations that attempted to recreate a sense of continuity with the pre-Partition past. Yet this nostalgic memory was not homogeneous; it was different by community, generation, and social location. For the initial generation of migrants, Partition was rupture and trauma, but for later generations who were born in host nations or post-Partition India, the event was redescribed in terms of family histories, media, and cultural representation, mythologized as an occasion of shared suffering and endurance.

Internationally, this culture of Partition migration had a deeply impacting influence on the character and development of the global Punjabi diaspora. When Punjabi migrants settled in nations such as the UK, Canada, and the US in the years after Partition, they brought not just economic ambition but also a shared memory of displacement. Diasporic communities created in the form of religious centres, cultural associations, and political activist groups frequently turned into sites for the preservation, contestation, or mobilization of Partition stories. For example, Sikh diaspora organizations in the West frequently reference the trauma of Partition alongside the later 1984 anti-Sikh violence in India to articulate a narrative of historical victimization and community resilience. This illustrates how diasporic identity is continuously shaped by the interplay of memory, migration, and politics.

Moreover, the trauma of Partition also catalysed an ethic of self-reliance and solidarity among Punjabi migrants. Community-based support networks, like *langars* (community kitchens), rotating credit associations, and caste-based welfare organizations, became key instruments for survival and integration both nationally and transnationally. Yet, the same institutions also sometimes helped reinforce conservative social hierarchies, such as caste divisions and patriarchal traditions, even in the putatively liberal environments of diaspora. This tension between community unity and internal ranking remains a characteristic element of post-Partition Punjabi diasporic existence.

The state also had a determinative influence on the shape of post-Partition migration and identity. In India, the resettlement of Punjabi refugees became a priority issue for the new government, which wanted to prove its legitimacy and ability to handle humanitarian emergencies. The Ministry of Relief and Rehabilitation and the Department of Refugee Rehabilitation managed the distribution of land, housing, and compensation, though these were usually bogged down in bureaucracy, corruption, and favouritism. State resources were not equally accessible, and caste and class continued to act as mediators of who benefited and who continued to be marginalised. However, the refugee experience also became a site of citizenship-making, as migrants interacted with state institutions, demanded entitlements, and, in doing so, rearticulated their relationship with the Indian nation-state.

In Pakistan, the conditions were just as complicated. Muslim refugees from East Punjab, popularly known as Muhajirs, were confronted with immense challenges to integrate into West Punjab and the rest of the newly created state. Even though they shared religious identity, they were often perceived as outsiders by indigenous populations, and tensions arose over land, employment, and representation. The Pakistani state initially idealized these migrants as monumental citizens of the new Islamic republic, but this rhetoric often failed to be translated into practical assistance, particularly for working-class or lower-caste Muslims who were discriminated against in social and bureaucratic systems. The Partition of India in 1947 was not just a piece of history but a deep sociological break that still influences the identities, practices, and dreams of the Punjabi diaspora. It compelled a reconstitution of community boundaries, reordered social hierarchies, and created a legacy of trauma and resilience that resonates across generations. The Partition migration experience laid bare the highly stratified character of society and demonstrated how big historical events have the potential to consolidate or reverse established power dynamics. By virtue of its continued influence on memory, mobility, and identity, Partition continues to be a dominant analytic category in any sociological examination of the Punjabi experience of migration.

5.2 Post-Independence Migration: Economic and Political Drivers

Post-independence migration among Punjabis was shaped by a combination of economic and political factors, which transformed the region's social fabric and created new patterns of transnational movement. The Green Revolution, which began in the 1960s, and the subsequent migration to Western countries and the Middle East, were pivotal in reshaping the socio-economic landscape of Punjab. From a sociological perspective, these phenomena can be understood as responses to structural changes in the economy, the globalization of labour markets, and the interplay of local and global forces that influence individual and collective decision-making.

The Green Revolution in Punjab, though initially celebrated as a success in development, also generated large socio-economic inequalities that led to both internal and international migration patterns. The use of high-yield variety (HYV) seeds, chemical fertilizers, and mechanized agriculture benefited disproportionately large and medium-scale landowners, most of whom were members of dominant castes such as the Jat Sikhs. Whereas these families were successful in generating excess wealth and reinvesting it in agribusiness or foreign migration, landless labourers and smallholders became progressively marginalized. The uneven distribution of returns from agriculture led to a dual economy in rural Punjab: one of relative affluence and the other of increasing poverty, indebtedness, and erosion of traditional means of livelihood. This division created a boom in desires among the rural middle class to pursue economic security overseas and an imperative for the lower rungs to seek migrant employment internally to urban areas or outside of India in search of wage employment.

Sociologically speaking, such migration was comprehensible in terms of push and pull factors, where economic stagnation, agrarian stress, and unemployment pushed out people, and the promise of remittances, social mobility, and transnational kinship networks pulled them in. Cultural discourses within Punjabi society also transformed to build migration as a desirable or even necessary strategy. International migration especially to places like Canada, the United Kingdom, and the United States became a status symbol, a sign of success, and a measure of modernity. It was not unusual for an entire village to have connections overseas, where migrants arranged for the entry of kin through marriage, student visas, or work contracts. These practices established transnational social fields networks of relationships and exchanges that linked migrants with their communities of origin and facilitated the ongoing circulation of capital, goods, ideas, and people.

The political climate in post-independence Punjab also facilitated migratory streams. The establishment of regional movements, such as calls for an independent Sikh state (Khalistan) throughout the 1980s, led to increased surveillance, militarization, and political tensions. Sikh youth, especially those considered to be tied to separatist politics, availed themselves of asylum in Western nations, making political instability an argument for seeking refugee status. These politically driven movements gave another texture to the Punjabi diaspora, where dissent and exile became constitutive of the experience of displacement. The international Sikh community, in return, became increasingly involved in advocating for minority rights and the acknowledgement of state repression in India, further cementing transnational political identities.

In addition, the contribution of remittances from foreign Punjabis started to increasingly influence local patterns of development. International migration-intensive villages saw increased consumerism, private schools, and infrastructural growth. The influx of capital also led to commodification of social life, such as dowries, marriage alliances, and caste-based networking for migration. In this regard, post-independence migration cannot be understood as purely economic it was just as much about reimagining mobility, status, and identity in an increasingly globalizing world

Green Revolution and Its Socio-economic Consequences

The Green Revolution, introduced in Punjab in the 1960s, was a state-led initiative aimed at increasing agricultural productivity through the adoption of high-yielding varieties (HYVs) of wheat and rice, chemical fertilizers, pesticides, and mechanized farming techniques. While it succeeded in making Punjab the "breadbasket of India", its socio-economic consequences were profound and multifaceted, leading to significant changes in rural society and migration patterns.

From a sociological perspective, the Green Revolution can be seen as a double-edged sword. On one hand, it brought prosperity to many farmers, particularly those who owned medium to large landholdings. The increased agricultural productivity led to higher incomes for these farmers, enabling them to invest in modern machinery, education, and consumer goods. This created a new class of affluent rural elites who became symbols of Punjab's agricultural success (Singh, 2001). However, the benefits of the Green Revolution were unevenly distributed, exacerbating existing inequalities within rural society.

Small and marginal farmers, who lacked the resources to invest in the new technologies, were often left behind. Many were forced to sell their land to larger landowners and became agricultural labourers or migrated to urban areas in search of work. This led to the proletarianization of a significant section of the rural population, as traditional agrarian relations were replaced by capitalist modes of production (Bhalla & Chadha, 1983). The Green Revolution also had ecological consequences, such as soil degradation and groundwater depletion, which further marginalized small farmers and labourers.

The Green Revolution also had a gendered impact on Punjabi society. While men primarily controlled the new agricultural technologies and resources, women were often relegated to unpaid or low-paid labour. This reinforced patriarchal structures and limited women's access to economic opportunities. At the same time, the increased income from agriculture enabled some families to invest in the education of their children, including daughters, leading to a gradual shift in gender roles and aspirations (Nijhawan, 2016).

The socio-economic changes brought about by the Green Revolution also had a direct impact on migration patterns. The prosperity of some farmers enabled them to send their children abroad for higher education, particularly to Western countries like Canada, the United Kingdom, and the United States. This created a culture of transnational migration, where education and employment abroad became aspirational goals for many Punjabi families. At the same time, the marginalization of small farmers and labourers pushed many to seek work in urban centres within India or abroad, particularly in the Middle East.

The effects of the Green Revolution on rural Punjab were more than just a rise in agricultural output. It created sweeping changes in social, economic, and demographic formations that reformed the very character of Punjabi society. As the larger landowners who were in a position to implement the new technologies quickly became wealthy, the smaller landowners were left behind, giving rise to a gap between the rural elite and the working poor. The agricultural revolution with the Green Revolution also brought large-scale changes to migration patterns as some Punjabis opted to migrate abroad in order to avail themselves of new opportunities, and others went for work in cities or the Middle East.

Concentration of resources among medium and large landholders facilitated them in concentrating economic as well as political power, thereby reinforcing the prevalence of these classes in local communities. These owners of land were in a position to invest in irrigation systems, farm machinery, and fertilizers, enhancing their agricultural production further. The accrued wealth also provided them with the economic capital to make investments in education and modern consumer items, creating a new rural bourgeoisie with a connection to world markets. This social stratification rendered the success of the Green Revolution visible at the community level, as the wealthy landowners came to represent the victory of modern agricultural techniques and capitalist progress. They also became the leading agents of local economic transformation, influencing the consumption habits and social aspirations of their communities (Singh, 2001).

Concurrently, marginalization of marginal and small farmers, who did not have the capital to engage in the Green Revolution, resulted in degradation of traditional farming livelihoods. While smaller farmers struggled to survive, numerous ones were compelled to sell their lands to larger landowners or relocate to urban areas in pursuit of alternative livelihoods. This transformation towards wage labour not only disturbed the old agrarian economy but also reorganized the rural social structure of Punjab. The proletarianization of agricultural workers, most of whom had been earlier involved in subsistence agriculture, led to an increased dependence on urban wage work or remittances from migrant family members who went abroad. This labour migration process, especially to the Western world and Middle East, assisted in maintaining the rural economy but also resulted in increased social disintegration (Bhalla & Chadha, 1983).

The ecological impact of the Green Revolution also contributed significantly towards influencing migration patterns. The extensive application of chemical fertilizers and pesticides, as well as excessive extraction of groundwater for irrigation purposes, resulted in extensive environmental degradation in most of Punjab. The fertility of the soil started to dwindle, and the exhaustion of water resources further taxed the agricultural yield of the area. Consequently, small farmers, who were already under economic stress, increasingly struggled to maintain their livelihoods. The environmental disaster added to rural household economic hardships and forced numerous families to find alternative means of sustenance. The increase in debt in the farm sector, accompanied by land degradation, caused emigration to towns or countries elsewhere to be more and more attractive for the families in the rural areas (Swarup, 2012).

There also existed a crucial role for the gendered processes in socio-economic changes ushered in through the Green Revolution. Although men chiefly dominated access to the new agriculture technologies and materials, women remained in low-level or unpaid occupations, mostly functioning as farm workers or performing housework. The economic contribution of women in several rural homes did not receive the recognition it needed, even if they contributed markedly to the support of agricultural production. The patriarchal gender relations supported by the Green Revolution resulted in women having limited access to the financial gains that resulted from agricultural productivity increases. Yet, the higher income from agriculture did provide new opportunities for certain women, especially in educational ambitions. In some families, the Green Revolution allowed women to seek higher education since the prosperity brought about by agriculture gave them the economic means to go to schools or colleges. This change in educational goals was a slow but significant shift in gender roles in the household and in Punjabi society at large (Nijhawan, 2016).

Concurrently, the economic prosperity of some rural families, especially those from more affluent farming backgrounds, enabled them to send their children overseas for higher education. The foreign migration of young women and men, mostly to nations such as Canada, the United States, and the United Kingdom, became a desirable aspiration for many rural Punjabis. This migration was not only economically motivated; it was driven by aspirations for upward mobility, modernity, and a better life for generations to come. The successful migration of one member of a family would often lead others to migrate, establishing transnational migration networks that expanded Punjab's economic and social reach beyond India's borders.

The socio-economic transformation initiated by the Green Revolution also initiated a transformation in the labour market. With the agricultural sector growing more capital-intensive and mechanized, the need for labour reduced, and the workers were left without a steady occupation. This led to rural-to-urban migration within India or overseas as a survival technique. Most of them searched for jobs in the Middle East, where shortages of unskilled labour in the construction sector and the oil industry provided openings for such employees. This movement to the Middle East, especially Saudi Arabia, the UAE, and Kuwait, served as a major source of income for the rural community and was responsible for supporting the economy of Punjab in the post-Green Revolution era. The remittances that these migrant workers sent back became an economic lifeline for many families, strengthening the bond between Punjab and the international economy even further.

Migration to Western Countries and the Middle East

The post-independence period also saw a significant increase in Punjabi migration to Western countries and the Middle East. This migration was driven by a combination of economic opportunities, political factors, and the globalization of labour markets. From a sociological perspective, this migration can be understood as a response to both "push" and "pull" factors, including economic disparities, political instability, and the demand for labour in industrialized and oil-rich economies.

Migration to Western countries, particularly Canada, the United Kingdom, and the United States, was often driven by the desire for better economic opportunities and higher education. Many Punjabi migrants to these countries were from the rural middle class, who used their agricultural wealth to finance their children's education abroad. This migration was often facilitated by social networks, as earlier migrants helped their relatives and friends settle in these countries. The establishment of Punjabi communities in these countries created a transnational network that supported further migration (Tatla, 1999).

The migration to Western countries also had a significant impact on Punjabi identity and culture. Migrants often sought to preserve their cultural heritage through the establishment of *gurdwaras*, cultural associations, and festivals. At the same time, they had to navigate the challenges of assimilation and discrimination in their host societies. This created a dual identity, where migrants were both rooted in their Punjabi heritage and influenced by the cultural norms of their host countries (Dusenbery, 1995).

Migration to the Middle East, particularly to countries like Saudi Arabia, the United Arab Emirates, and Kuwait, was driven by the demand for labour in the construction, oil, and service sectors. This migration was often temporary, with workers returning to Punjab after a few years. However, it had a significant impact on the socio-economic structure of Punjabi society. Remittances from Middle Eastern migrants became an important source of income for many families, enabling them to invest in agriculture, education, and housing (Nayyar, 1994).

The migration to the Middle East also had a gendered dimension, as it was primarily men who migrated for work, leaving women to manage households and agricultural activities in their absence. This led to changes in gender roles and family dynamics, as women took on greater responsibilities and gained more autonomy in decision-making. At the same time, the absence of male family members created new challenges, such as increased workloads and social isolation for women (Gamburd, 2000).

From a sociological perspective, the migration to Western countries and the Middle East can be seen as part of a broader process of globalization, where the movement of labour is shaped by global economic forces and local social structures. This migration has created new forms of transnationalism, where migrants maintain strong ties to their homeland while also integrating into their host societies. It has also led to the emergence of a global Punjabi diaspora, which plays an important role in shaping the cultural, economic, and political landscape of Punjab and its migrant communities.

5.3 Formation of Transnational Networks

The formation of transnational networks among the Punjabi diaspora is a complex sociological phenomenon that reflects the interplay of identity, culture, and globalization. These networks are sustained and strengthened through diaspora organizations and cultural associations, which play a critical role in maintaining connections between migrants and their homeland, fostering a sense of community abroad, and facilitating the exchange of resources, ideas, and cultural practices. From a sociological perspective, these organizations are not merely social clubs but are instrumental in shaping the diasporic experience, negotiating identities, and addressing the challenges of living in transnational spaces.

The creation of transnational networks amongst the Punjabi diaspora is a central theme of the more general process of migration and globalization. These national-transcending networks are more than a scattered aggregation of diaspora communities; they are changing systems of economic, social, and cultural interaction that assist in maintaining the welfare and identity of diaspora group members. A characteristic of these networks is that they can overcome the constraints of time and space, establishing new patterns of connectivity that enable the flow of people, ideas, and resources between the homeland and the diaspora. Within the context of the Punjabi diaspora, these networks have been crucial to the reproduction of cultural practice, the negotiation of identity, and the formation of new identities of belonging.

At the heart of the development of these transnational networks are diaspora organizations and cultural associations, which act as the primary institutions that connect the Punjabi diaspora to its homeland. These organizations tend to arise as a reaction to the specific challenges that migrants experience as they try to integrate into their host communities while at the same time holding on to their origins. These organizations, whether they are cultural preservation, social welfare, or religious practice organizations, assist in creating a sense of community for people who are usually spread out in different locations. They provide sites for sociality and cultural exchange where members can share experiences, provide mutual support, and celebrate their common heritage.

Sociologically, these diaspora groups are neither simple social nor cultural clubs. They serve as intermediaries that mediate the negotiation of identities, enabling members of the Punjabi diaspora to navigate the complexity of living in a transnational space. Most members of the diaspora are torn between two worlds, attempting to reconcile their national or ethnic identity with the expectations of their host culture. These groups are important in assisting individuals in reconciling this duality by offering a means of cultural expression, religious practice, and reinforcement of traditional values. For example, most Sikh diaspora communities overseas have opened *gurdwaras* (places of worship) that are not just religious institutions but also serve as centres of culture, where people can participate in community activities, observe traditional festivals, and preserve linguistic relationships through language courses and cultural events.

In addition, the transnational networks are also important in solving the social and economic issues that are associated with diaspora communities. One of the primary roles of diaspora organizations is to act as facilitators of remittances and foreign financial assistance to the homeland. Through the money sent by migrants to their relatives, these financial flows become a major vehicle for financing economic growth in the homeland. Remittances may be utilized for various purposes, ranging from financing education and healthcare to financing small enterprise and agricultural growth. In this manner, diaspora networks play an important role in ensuring that economic linkages between the Punjabi diaspora and Punjab are sustained, establishing a type of transnational economic connectedness.

Resource exchange, which encompasses knowledge and skills, is yet another vital element of these networks. There are numerous highly educated people among the Punjabi diaspora with valuable skills in demand in the host countries. These skills, when carried back to the country via diaspora networks, can be used for local development and the enhancement of sectors like education, healthcare, and technology. For instance, the increasing number of Punjabis in the international information technology industry has resulted in the growth of knowledge-sharing networks that enable the repatriation of technical skills and expertise back to India, especially Punjab. This exchange of information establishes a dynamic connection between diaspora and homeland and tightens the bond between the two further.

Besides economic and cultural interaction, there is also a substantial political aspect to the creation of transnational networks among the Punjabi diaspora. Such networks tend to act as platforms for political action, where diaspora members mobilize around issues regarding their homeland. Political campaigning and lobbying, be it on human rights, agricultural issues, or political representation, are frequently mobilized through these diaspora groups. For example, when there was political turmoil in Punjab in the 1980s, the Punjabi diaspora in Canada, the United Kingdom, and the United States of

America contributed significantly to lobbying on behalf of Sikhs in India. These transnational political networks facilitated the international focus on the concerns of the Punjabi community, illustrating how diaspora organizations are able to exert influence beyond their immediate local contexts.

In addition, these networks offer a platform for identity preservation and redefinition. As the members of the Punjabi diaspora settle into new cultural settings, the issue of what it is to be Punjabi, Sikh, or Indian becomes salient. These transnational networks make the negotiation of these identities possible, allowing for tradition to be maintained as well as adapted to new political and social realities. The transnational nature of these networks allows the members of the diaspora to constantly be connected with their history and culture, developing a flexible, dynamic sense of identity that escapes the constrictions of geographic borders.

Role of Diaspora Organizations and Cultural Associations

Diaspora organizations and cultural associations serve as vital nodes in the transnational networks of the Punjabi diaspora. These organizations are often established to address the specific needs of migrant communities, such as preserving cultural heritage, providing social support, and advocating for political and economic rights. They act as bridges between the homeland and the host country, enabling migrants to maintain a sense of belonging to Punjab while navigating the complexities of their new environments.

One of the primary functions of these organizations is cultural preservation. In the face of assimilation pressures in host countries, Punjabi diaspora organizations work to keep cultural traditions are kept alive through festivals, language classes, and religious activities. For example, *gurdwaras* (Sikh temples) in countries like Canada, the United Kingdom, and the United

States serve not only as places of worship but also as community centres where Punjabi language, music, and cuisine are celebrated (Dusenbery, 1995). These spaces provide a sense of continuity and stability for migrants, especially second-generation youth who may feel disconnected from their cultural roots.

Cultural associations also play a significant role in fostering solidarity and collective identity among diaspora members. Organizations such as the World Punjabi Organization and the National Federation of Indian American Associations (NFIA) bring together Punjabis from diverse backgrounds to celebrate shared heritage and address common challenges. These associations often organize events such as Punjabi literary conferences, sports tournaments, and cultural festivals, which strengthen social bonds and create a sense of unity among diaspora members (Sharma, 2011). From a sociological perspective, these activities help to construct a transnational Punjabi identity that transcends geographic boundaries.

In addition to cultural preservation, diaspora organizations are deeply involved in political and economic advocacy. They often lobby host governments on issues such as immigration policies, anti-discrimination laws, and minority rights. For instance, Punjabi organizations in Canada have been instrumental in advocating for the recognition of Sikh religious symbols, such as the *kirpan*, and in addressing issues of racial profiling and hate crimes (Tatla, 1999). These efforts highlight the role of diaspora organizations as agents of social change, both in the host country and in the homeland.

Diaspora organizations also facilitate economic and developmental ties between Punjab and its migrant communities. Many organizations channel remittances and investments into development projects in Punjab, such as schools, hospitals, and infrastructure. For example, the NRI Sabha (Non-Resident Indian Association) in Punjab works closely with diaspora members to identify and fund projects that address local needs (Axel, 2001). These initiatives not only contribute to the economic development of Punjab but also reinforce the emotional and material connections between migrants and their homeland.

From a sociological perspective, the role of diaspora organizations and cultural associations can be understood through the lens of transnationalism, which emphasizes the fluid and dynamic nature of migrant identities and connections. These organizations enable migrants to navigate the dualities of their existence being rooted in their cultural heritage while adapting to the realities of their host societies. They also highlight the agency of migrants in shaping their own diasporic experiences, as they actively create and sustain networks that transcend national boundaries.

The function of diaspora organizations and cultural associations in the Punjabi diaspora is multifaceted, bridging the homeland-migrant communities' gap while fostering a dynamic process of cultural preservation, political lobbying, economic growth, and social cohesion. They are vital not only as community spaces, but also as spaces for change where migrants are able to negotiate their own identities, experience their cultural heritage, and help their host society as well as their country of origin. Above their role as a repository for culture, they also offer indispensable support systems for diasporic communities that provide solidarity and strength.

One of the most crucial roles that are played by diaspora organizations is that of preserving cultures. Under pressure to assimilate into host societies, particularly in the second generation, these institutions keep alive the cultural practices which the migrants retain and desire to pass on. They assist in the maintenance of the use of the Punjabi language, the observance of religious rituals, and the celebration of cultural festivals. In the diaspora, *gurdwaras* a typically taken to be the very foundation of Sikh existence are utilized dually. Although they are religious centres, they also serve as community centres where Punjabi culture is maintained. Daily classes in Punjabi language, religious studies, and music, including playing traditional instruments, are part of these centres. These activities not only enable migrants to keep in touch with their heritage but also enable younger generations to discover their roots, allowing them to feel part of the wider transnational Punjabi community (Dusenbery, 1995).

Cultural affiliations also serve as social glue, uniting people who would otherwise be disconnected from each other. Such organizations offer a common platform for identity-building, essential in fostering solidarity among heterogeneous members of the Punjabi diaspora. For example, activities like literary conferences, Punjabi movie screenings, and sporting events act as channels for reaffirming a common sense of belongingness. Such events cut across regional, caste, and class cleavages in the diaspora, producing a collective identity as one. Through joint participation, migrants who may be scattered over vast distances in other countries can re-establish their connection with their fellow Punjabis, establishing their position within a larger, transnational community. Social interactions during these events define Punjabi-ness outside Punjab, setting up a fluid, flexible identity that is able to modify its structure in conformity with the altering social and cultural landscapes of host nations (Sharma, 2011).

But the activities of diaspora organizations go beyond cultural life. The organizations have been actively engaged in political and social activism that directly influences the members' lives. Punjabi diaspora groups, in nations such as Canada, the United States, and the United Kingdom, have been at the centre of campaigns regarding immigration issues, religious freedoms, and minority rights. For instance, groups like the Canadian

Sikh Coalition have worked aggressively to promote the right of Sikh Canadians to carry the *kirpan* (a ceremonial dagger) in public places, citing the value of religious freedom. Likewise, Punjabi groups have played a key role in working against racial profiling and hate crimes, noting the specific issues that Sikhs and Punjabis encounter outside their home countries. These advocacy campaigns show the ability of diaspora organizations to shape policy, counter discrimination, and advance the rights of minority groups in their host nations (Tatla, 1999).

Apart from political advocacy, diaspora organizations enable important economic and developmental linkages between the diaspora and Punjab. Diaspora organizations tend to serve as channels for remittances, investments, and development initiatives. Remittances transferred by migrants are perhaps the most concrete means through which the diaspora contributes to the economic prosperity of their native place. Diaspora organizations facilitate the transfer of these remittances to development projects that have a direct effect on Punjabi communities at large. For example, the NRI Sabha (Non-Resident Indian Association) in Punjab is instrumental in selecting and financing development projects, such as building schools, hospitals, and infrastructure projects that enhance the quality of life in rural and urban areas of the state. These projects highlight the economic function that diaspora organizations have in promoting development and having strong material connections to their homeland (Axel, 2001).

Sociologically, diaspora organizations can be explained in terms of transnationalism, a theory that highlights the fluid and interconnected character of migrant identities and experiences. Transnationalism argues that migration is not a singular event but a continuous, dynamic process that cuts across several countries, cultures, and communities. Diaspora organizations, in this regard, play a central role in facilitating transnational identities by offering resources and spaces that allow migrants to remain connected to their home country while settling into their host communities. Diaspora organizations assist migrants in negotiating the challenges of living between two or more worlds so that they can settle into new socio-political worlds without fully disconnecting from their heritage. In addition, these organizations also demonstrate the migrants' own agency in building their own diasporic identities, as they engage actively in creating and maintaining networks without boundaries across nations.

By engaging in preserving their culture, advocating politically, and developing economically, diaspora organizations contribute to evolving a type of global citizenship among the Punjabi migrants. They offer not only a sense of belonging but also a sense of responsibility towards both their host nation and their place of origin. These organizations indicate the dynamic character of identity today in the globalized world, where people are no longer restricted to negotiating singular affiliation but can negotiate multiple attachments, juxtaposing their ethnic background with their future in their host society. Through these efforts, they help shape a transnational Punjabi identity that cuts across space and is regularly reworked according to changing social, cultural, and political realities.

6

Socio-political Role of the Punjabi Diaspora in Punjab

6.1 Advocacy for Socio-political Reforms

The Punjabi diaspora, particularly its second and third generations, has emerged as a significant force in advocating for socio-political reforms in Punjab. Their unique position as global citizens with deep-rooted connections to their ancestral homeland allows them to bridge local and global perspectives, bringing innovative ideas and resources to address governance challenges. From a sociological perspective, the diaspora's role in socio-political advocacy can be understood through frameworks such as transnationalism, social capital, and global citizenship. This section explores the diaspora's contributions to addressing governance challenges in Punjab, supported by case studies of diaspora-led initiatives, and examines how these efforts contribute to nation-building in contemporary contexts.

The Punjabi diaspora's call for socio-political changes in Punjab is an active crossroads of transnational participation and domestic governance. Whereas migration has traditionally represented some sort of departure or alienation, the modern Punjabi diaspora shows that physical distance does not have to mean political detachment. Instead, the growing transnational linkages have allowed diaspora individuals particularly the educated second and third generations to remain significantly active in Punjab's socio-political process through direct and indirect participation.

Among the prime movers of such engagement is the diaspora's social capital build-up and familiarity with democratic institutions and governance models in host nations such as Canada, the United Kingdom, and the United States. These learnings tend to shape their agendas for change back home. Diaspora members constantly criticize such phenomena as political corruption, bureaucratic incompetence, and ecological degradation in Punjab, for example. Their global positionality as citizens in their host nations with access to resources and institutions enables them to organize efforts that may be infeasible for grassroots actors back home because of institutional barriers or fear of political persecution.

An excellent example of such engagement includes support for initiatives of clean governance, like election transparency campaigns, anti-corruption campaigns, and citizen empowerment on digital platforms. Diaspora-financed NGOs such as the Punjab Lok Sujag and Sanjh Punjab have made efforts to raise awareness regarding the right to information, environmental sustainability, and civic responsibility. Diaspora professionals such as academics, lawyers, and journalists, who provide global insights and best practices, benefit these organizations either through money or intellectual contributions.

On the environmental activism front, the Punjabi diaspora has been vocal regarding the environmental crisis that is taking place in Punjab as a result of groundwater depletion, chemical-based farming, and air pollution due to stubble burning.

Initiatives led by the diaspora have advocated for sustainable farming practices and backed grassroots environmental movements in Punjab. For instance, organizations like EcoSikh, which emerged from diaspora communities, have worked with local stakeholders to encourage tree planting campaigns, water conservation, and organic cultivation. This is a type of transnational environmentalism where diasporic actors are involved in ecological reforms while negotiating their identity and responsibility toward their homeland.

Diaspora's Role in Addressing Governance Challenges

(i) Transnational Advocacy and Policy Influence

The Punjabi diaspora plays a crucial role in advocating for policy reforms and good governance in Punjab. Leveraging their education, professional expertise, and global networks, diaspora members often act as intermediaries between local communities and international organizations, advocating for transparency, accountability, and inclusive development. For instance, diaspora-led organizations have been instrumental in raising awareness about issues such as environmental degradation, agricultural distress, and human rights violations in Punjab.

From a sociological perspective, this transnational advocacy can be analysed through the lens of transnationalism, which emphasizes the interconnectedness of diasporic communities across national borders. By engaging in advocacy, the diaspora not only addresses local governance challenges but also fosters a sense of global citizenship, where individuals take responsibility for the well-being of their ancestral homeland.

This type of transnational advocacy also portrays the changing dynamics of diaspora engagement, wherein individuals and groups are no longer mere benefactors but responsible stakeholders in their country's political and development discourse. Diaspora members tend to leverage their credibility and exposure to global forums like human rights forums, academe, and transnational NGOs to put the spotlight on governance malfeasance and urge authorities to make reforms. These initiatives are often made easier by digital media, which has opened up opportunities for instant communication and mobilization across borders, thus giving a louder voice to the diaspora in policy-making in Punjab.

In addition, this advocacy is not only critical but also entails suggesting and advocating alternative models of governance based on democratic principles, social justice, and sustainability. For example, diaspora-funded think tanks and civic organizations tend to work with local stakeholders to undertake policy research, pilot new programmes, and train local leaders. These interventions, based on both global best practices and local expertise, enrich the policy environment in Punjab. Consequently, the diaspora is presented as a transnational actor whose activism adds to developmental outcomes as well as to reinforcing democratic institutions and participatory democracy in the region.

(ii) Mobilizing Social and Financial Capital

The diaspora's access to social and financial capital enables them to support socio-political reforms in Punjab. Many diaspora members contribute financially to grassroots organizations, political movements, and development projects aimed at improving governance and public services. For example, diaspora-funded initiatives have supported education, healthcare, and infrastructure development in rural Punjab, addressing systemic inequalities and improving the quality of life for local communities.

Bourdieu's (1986) concept of social capital is particularly relevant here, as it highlights the importance of networks, relationships, and resources in achieving collective goals. By mobilizing their social and financial capital, the diaspora strengthens local institutions and empowers communities to advocate for their rights and interests.

Besides straight financial support, the Punjabi diaspora also mobilizes professional networks and institutional connections to transfer skills, legitimacy, and innovativeness to grassroots reform activities. These assets are usually funnelled through institutionalized NGOs, personal community groups, or direct linkages with village-level institutions. Several second- and third-generation diaspora members, especially those in transnational professions like medicine, teaching, engineering, and public policy, give back their time and expertise through short-term missions or distant mentoring, thus investing in human capital in their countries of origin. Such involvement indicates a deepening of the diaspora's commitment from charity-based to sustainable development and empowerment.

In addition, diaspora philanthropy tends to be followed by a critical sensitivity to governance deficits and an interest in promoting accountability in the host country's administration. Some diaspora communities have even established monitoring systems for the utilization of donated funds, promoting transparency and participatory planning. In such practice, the diaspora is not only contributing to material development, but also to the development of civic values, democratic engagement, and institutional responsiveness. Bourdieu's (1986) focus on the transformative power of social capital is evident here, as the diaspora's relational networks facilitate new modes of political and civic participation, supporting a bottom-up strategy to socio-political change in Punjab.

(iii) Promoting Civic Engagement and Political Participation

The diaspora also plays a vital role in promoting civic engagement and political participation in Punjab. Through awareness campaigns, workshops, and digital platforms, diaspora organizations encourage Punjabis to actively participate in democratic processes, such as voting, community organizing, and policy advocacy. This is particularly important in a context where political apathy and disenfranchisement are prevalent.

From a sociological perspective, this emphasis on civic engagement reflects the principles of participatory democracy, where individuals and communities play an active role in shaping their political and social environments. By fostering a culture of participation, the diaspora contributes to the democratization of governance in Punjab.

Aside from online campaigning and educational movements, the Punjabi diaspora has also widely utilized social media and transnational communication networks to share vital information and raise political consciousness among the citizenry of Punjab. Diaspora-operated YouTube channels, WhatsApp groups, and independent news websites frequently post counter-narratives and fact-checks against mainstream political rhetoric, thus making citizens aware of information that local media often omits. This online activism increases political literacy and assists in breaking misinformation cycles and voter disengagement.

Additionally, diaspora groups often work with local civil society stakeholders to organize town hall meetings, civic education campaigns, and training sessions that develop leadership skills and empower marginalized groups, particularly women and youth, to assume participatory roles in governance. These interventions not only activate local political engagement but also promote critical consciousness, whereby people start to perceive themselves as active agents of transformation instead of passive recipients of state policy. The diaspora's impact in advancing participatory democracy is especially relevant in areas traditionally marked by elite politics and clientelism. By expanding the civic base of participation, the Punjabi diaspora performs a transformative function in remaking political culture, promoting accountability, and strengthening democratic values at the grassroots level.

Case Studies of Diaspora-led Initiatives

1. *Environmental Advocacy: The Fight Against Punjab's Water Crisis*

Punjab's water crisis, characterized by depleting groundwater levels and widespread pollution, has been a major focus of diaspora-led advocacy. Organizations such as the Punjab Water Forum, founded by diaspora members, have been at the forefront of raising awareness about the crisis and advocating for sustainable water management practices.

The Punjab Water Forum has collaborated with local farmers, policymakers, and international experts to promote water conservation techniques, such as drip irrigation and crop diversification. These efforts have not only addressed the immediate challenges of water scarcity but also highlighted the need for long-term policy reforms to ensure sustainable development.

From a sociological perspective, this initiative exemplifies the diaspora's role as a bridge between local and global knowledge systems. By leveraging their expertise and networks, diaspora members facilitate the exchange of ideas and resources, enabling local communities to adopt innovative solutions to complex problems.

2. *Education and Empowerment: The Role of Diaspora-Funded Schools*

Education is another area where the diaspora has made significant contributions to socio-political reforms in Punjab. Diaspora-funded schools, such as those established by the Sikh Foundation and other community organizations, provide quality education to underprivileged children, particularly in rural areas. These schools not only focus on academic excellence but also emphasize values such as social justice, equality, and civic responsibility.

For example, the Sikh Foundation's schools have introduced innovative curricula that incorporate Punjabi language, history, and culture, fostering a sense of identity and pride among students. Additionally, these schools often serve as community hubs, offering adult education programmes, vocational training, and health services.

From a sociological perspective, these initiatives reflect the diaspora's commitment to social capital and community development. By investing in education, the diaspora empowers individuals and communities to challenge systemic inequalities and advocate for their rights, thereby contributing to the democratization of society.

3. *Human Rights Advocacy: Addressing Gender-based Violence*

The diaspora has also been actively involved in advocating for human rights, particularly in addressing gender-based violence in Punjab. Organizations such as the Punjab Women's Rights Initiative, founded by diaspora members, work to raise awareness about issues such as domestic violence, female infanticide, and gender discrimination.

Through campaigns, workshops, and legal aid services, these organizations empower women to assert their rights and challenge patriarchal norms. For instance, the Punjab Women's Rights Initiative has collaborated with local NGOs to establish shelters and support services for survivors of domestic violence, providing them with a safe space and access to resources.

From a sociological perspective, this advocacy reflects the principles of feminist theory, which emphasizes the importance of challenging systemic oppression and promoting gender equality. By addressing gender-based violence, the diaspora contributes to the creation of a more just and equitable society in Punjab.

Aside from offering direct support services, diaspora-led responses to gender-based violence in Punjab also target structural change by advancing legal reform as well as sensitizing the public. Such diaspora-led efforts tend to engage local lawyers, educators, and policymakers to empower legal frameworks supporting women's rights, making these laws more implementable, including the Protection of Women from Domestic Violence Act (2005). Advocacy movements often resist the normalization of gender violence by countering deeply ingrained cultural practices such as dowry, son preference, and stigmatization of survivors.

In addition, the Punjabi diaspora, second-generation feminists in particular, deploy international discourses of gender justice to frame agendas in Punjab. They introduce transnational frames of reference for local concerns, leveraging inclusive narratives of bodily autonomy, consent, and intersectionality. Their work creates solidarity among women in Punjab and other global feminist movements, creating a feedback loop that enhances local resistance and international mobilization. They give tools for empowerment as well as change public awareness about gender norms.

By reinforcing the voice of marginalized people and promoting a gender-equitable culture, the diaspora acts as a change-agent in ending patriarchy. Through their interventions, they engage in feminist praxis, stressing individual and political transformation, and work constructively toward a more equal and democratic Punjab.

Impact on Nation-Building

The socio-political advocacy of the Punjabi diaspora has significant implications for nation-building in contemporary contexts. By addressing governance challenges, promoting civic engagement, and empowering marginalized communities, the diaspora contributes to the development of a more inclusive and democratic society. Their efforts reflect the principles of global citizenship, where individuals take responsibility for the well-being of their communities and contribute to the collective good.

In today's globalized world, the role of younger generations in nation-building is deeply intertwined with their efforts to promote socio-political reforms. By leveraging their education, expertise, and networks, they create a sense of unity and purpose that transcends national borders. These efforts not only address immediate challenges but also foster long-term resilience and sustainability, shaping the future of nation-building in the 21st century.

The socio-political role of the Punjabi diaspora in advocating for reforms in Punjab is a testament to their commitment to their ancestral homeland and their vision for a more just and equitable society. Through transnational advocacy, mobilization of resources, and promotion of civic engagement, they address governance challenges and empower communities to shape their futures. These efforts not only contribute to the development of Punjab but also reflect the interconnectedness of global and local identities in a rapidly changing world. By embracing their dual roles as global citizens and cultural ambassadors, the diaspora plays a vital role in shaping the future of nation-building in the 21st century.

6.2 Influence on Policy-making and Local Development

The Punjabi diaspora, particularly its second and third generations, has increasingly become a significant actor in influencing policy-making and driving local development in Punjab. Their engagement with both state and non-state actors, coupled with their access to global networks and resources, enables them to address critical issues such as education, healthcare, and rural development. From a sociological perspective, this influence can be understood through frameworks such as transnationalism, social capital, and participatory development. This section delves into the diaspora's engagement with state and non-state actors and examines their impact on key areas of local development, highlighting their contributions to nation-building in contemporary contexts.

Over the past few years, the Punjabi diaspora's contribution to local development has moved beyond philanthropy to encompass strategic involvement in policy-making processes. Several diaspora members, especially professionals and businesspeople in nations such as Canada, the UK, and the US, have worked together with state agencies and NGOs in Punjab to co-develop and deliver development projects. These range from infrastructure development, education reform, rural skill development programmes, and public health programmes. Their exposure to international best practices and technologies improves the quality and innovativeness of such initiatives.

This interaction is typically placed within participatory development frameworks, where local populations are engaged in needs identification and solution formulation. Diaspora actors act as facilitators who connect global knowledge and local knowledge. Their social capital, established through networks of trust and shared identity, enables them to mobilize resources and negotiate local bureaucracies efficiently (Putnam, 2000). Additionally, their external status can provide credibility and mobilize additional support from international institutions.

From a sociological perspective, this is evidence of a move away from imposed top-down models of development to more reflexive and collaborative practice based on common heritage and mutual responsibility. By shaping policy-making and promoting sustainable local development, the Punjabi diaspora reinforces state-society relations as much as it remakes their own identity as transnational agents of transformation.

Engagement with State and Non-State Actors

(a) Collaboration with State Actors

The Punjabi diaspora's engagement with state actors, including government agencies and policy-makers, has been instrumental in shaping development policies in Punjab. By leveraging their expertise, networks, and financial resources, diaspora members often act as advisors, consultants, and advocates for policy reforms. For instance, diaspora-led organizations have collaborated with the Punjab government to design and implement programmes aimed at improving public services, such as education and healthcare.

One notable example is the Punjab Governance Reforms Commission, which includes diaspora members who bring global best practices to the table. Their contributions have led to the adoption of innovative policies, such as the use of technology in governance (e-governance) and the decentralization of administrative functions to improve service delivery at the grassroots level.

From a sociological perspective, this collaboration reflects the principles of participatory governance, where diverse stakeholders, including diaspora members, are involved in decision-making processes. By engaging with state actors, the diaspora ensures that development policies are inclusive, transparent, and responsive to the needs of local communities.

This increasing engagement between the Punjabi diaspora and the state represents a revolutionary change in development governance. In addition to providing economic assistance, diaspora individuals actively share intellectual capital—varied from bureaucratic innovations to sectoral expertise in such fields as healthcare and digital governance. Diaspora professionals included in institutions such as the Punjab Governance Reforms Commission both legitimize these organizations and facilitate cross-fertilization of ideas between Punjab and global policy networks.

These interactions tend to concentrate on capacity development within the state machinery itself. For instance, diaspora-initiated efforts have facilitated the introduction of citizen-oriented models of service delivery, de-bureaucratization, and transparency through e-governance platforms. These changes are designed to foster trust between the state and citizens particularly in rural and marginalized areas by enhancing the accessibility and accountability of public institutions.

On the sociological plane, this event represents a transition towards networked governance, under which non-traditional political actors like diasporas take part in deciding state policies. It also portrays a changing conceptualization of citizenship—one that operates beyond territorial limitations and accepts transnational engagement. The diaspora thus becomes a proactive stakeholder in Punjab's developmental destiny, not just via remittances or charity, but through steady, institutional partnerships that bring international wisdom to intersect with local know-how.

(b) Partnerships with Non-State Actors

In addition to state actors, the Punjabi diaspora actively collaborates with non-state actors, such as non-governmental organizations (NGOs), community-based organizations (CBOs), and international development agencies. These partnerships enable the diaspora to address complex socio-economic challenges that require multi-stakeholder approaches.

For example, diaspora-funded NGOs like the Punjab Rural Development Foundation work closely with local communities to implement development projects focused on education, healthcare, and livelihood generation. These projects often involve capacity-building initiatives, such as training programmes for teachers, healthcare workers, and farmers, empowering local communities to take ownership of their development.

From a sociological perspective, these partnerships exemplify the concept of social capital, where networks and relationships are leveraged to achieve collective goals. By working with non-state actors, the diaspora strengthens local institutions and fosters a sense of community ownership, which is essential for sustainable development.

These diaspora-non-state actor partnerships highlight the growing relevance of decentralized development approaches. Diaspora-NGO/CBO partnerships tend to bypass bureaucratic obstacles present in state-sponsored initiatives, allowing for more flexible and locally nuanced interventions. By financing and engaging in grassroots initiatives, the diaspora not only addresses vital resource gaps but also co-produces development with host communities. This participatory method promotes inclusivity, increases the legitimacy of projects, and makes sure that interventions are informed by the lived experiences of beneficiaries.

For example, efforts initiated by diaspora-funded agencies like the Punjab Rural Development Foundation have resulted in the opening up of mobile health clinics, vocational training centres, and women's cooperatives in underprivileged localities. Such activities are often developed in association with local constituents, reflecting bottom-up development and empowerment principles (Banks & Hulme, 2012).

Sociologically, such practices fit Bourdieu's (1986) concept of social capital, under which relationships that are founded on trust and have common social norms create networks to enable cooperative action. These collaborations create two-way relationships between the migrants and their home country, not only economically but socially, in terms of institution-building and social innovation. Such interactions reinforce the development projects' sustainability through integrating them in local social milieus and enhancing collective agency.

Impact on Education, Healthcare, and Rural Development

(i) Education: Bridging the Gap in Access and Quality

Education is a key area where the Punjabi diaspora has made significant contributions to local development in Punjab. Recognizing the importance of education as a driver of social and economic mobility, diaspora members have established schools, scholarships, and mentorship programmes to improve access to quality education for underprivileged children.

For instance, the Sikh Human Development Foundation, a diaspora-led organization, has set up schools in rural Punjab that provide free education to children from marginalized communities. These schools not only focus on academic excellence but also emphasize values such as social justice, equality, and civic responsibility. Additionally, the foundation offers scholarships for higher education, enabling students to pursue their dreams and contribute to the development of their communities.

From a sociological perspective, these initiatives reflect the diaspora's commitment to human capital development, which is essential for breaking the cycle of poverty and inequality. By investing in education, the diaspora empowers individuals and communities to challenge systemic barriers and advocate for their rights, thereby contributing to the democratization of society.

(ii) Healthcare: Improving Access and Quality of Care

The Punjabi diaspora has also played a crucial role in addressing healthcare challenges in Punjab, particularly in rural areas where access to quality healthcare is limited. Diaspora-funded healthcare initiatives, such as mobile clinics, telemedicine services, and health awareness campaigns, have significantly improved the health outcomes of local communities.

One notable example is the Punjab Health Initiative, a diaspora-led project that provides free healthcare services to underserved populations. The initiative includes mobile health units that travel to remote villages, offering diagnostic services, treatment, and health education. Additionally, the project collaborates with local healthcare providers to build their capacity and improve the quality of care.

From a sociological perspective, these healthcare initiatives reflect the principles of social justice and equity, where access to healthcare is recognized as a fundamental human right. By addressing healthcare disparities, the diaspora contributes to the creation of a more inclusive and equitable society in Punjab.

(iii) Rural Development: Empowering Communities for Sustainable Growth

Rural development is another area where the Punjabi diaspora has made significant contributions. Recognizing the challenges faced by rural communities, such as poverty, unemployment, and lack of infrastructure, diaspora members have implemented projects aimed at improving livelihoods and promoting sustainable development.

For example, the Punjab Agricultural Development Programme, funded by the diaspora, focuses on promoting sustainable farming practices, such as organic farming and water conservation. The programme provides farmers with training, resources, and market linkages, enabling them to increase their productivity and income. Additionally, the programme includes initiatives to improve rural infrastructure, such as roads, irrigation systems, and community centres, enhancing the quality of life for rural communities.

From a sociological perspective, these rural development initiatives reflect the principles of participatory development, where local communities are actively involved in the planning and implementation of development projects. By empowering rural communities, the diaspora fosters a sense of ownership and agency, which is essential for sustainable development.

These diaspora-led rural development initiatives illustrate a strategic shift from charity-based interventions to empowerment-driven models of development. By integrating local knowledge systems with global best practices, these projects create pathways for sustainable livelihoods that are environmentally sound and socially inclusive. Programmes like the Punjab Agricultural Development Programme not only enhance agricultural productivity through sustainable methods but also mitigate the long-term ecological degradation caused by the Green Revolution such as groundwater depletion and soil erosion (Singh, 2009).

Furthermore, diaspora involvement often brings innovation to rural governance structures. For instance, participatory rural appraisal (PRA) techniques are increasingly employed to ensure that community voices are central in identifying needs and shaping interventions. This aligns with the paradigm of "development from below", emphasizing that community empowerment and collective action are prerequisites for durable progress (Chambers, 1997).

From a sociological lens, these efforts resonate with the concept of "capability enhancement" as proposed by Sen (1999), where development is viewed as the expansion of people's freedoms and abilities to lead lives they value. By funding infrastructure, training, and market access, the diaspora enhances the social and economic agency of rural populations, thus contributing to long-term structural transformation in Punjab's countryside.

Impact on Nation-Building

The influence of the Punjabi diaspora on policy-making and local development has significant implications for nation-building in contemporary contexts. By engaging with state and non-state actors, the diaspora ensures that development policies are inclusive, transparent, and responsive to the needs of local communities. Their contributions to education, healthcare, and rural development not only address immediate challenges but also foster long-term resilience and sustainability, shaping the future of nation-building in the 21st century.

In today's globalized world, the role of younger generations in nation-building is deeply intertwined with their efforts to promote socio-economic development. By leveraging their education, expertise, and networks, they create a sense of unity and purpose that transcends national borders. These efforts not only address immediate challenges but also foster long-term resilience and sustainability, shaping the future of nation-building in the 21st century.

The influence of the Punjabi diaspora on policy-making and local development is a testament to their commitment to their ancestral homeland and their vision for a more just and equitable society. Through their engagement with state and non-state actors, they address critical issues such as education, healthcare, and rural development, empowering communities to shape their futures. These efforts not only contribute to the development of Punjab but also reflect the interconnectedness of global and local identities in a rapidly changing world. By embracing their dual roles as global citizens and cultural ambassadors, the diaspora plays a vital role in shaping the future of nation-building in the 21st century.

6.3 Challenges and Criticisms

While the Punjabi diaspora has made significant contributions to socio-political reforms and local development in Punjab, their engagement is not without challenges and criticisms. These limitations stem from structural, cultural, and political factors that complicate the diaspora's ability to effect meaningful change. From a sociological perspective, these challenges can be understood through frameworks such as transnationalism, power dynamics, and cultural hybridity.

This section explores the limitations of diaspora engagement in socio-political reforms, highlighting the complexities and contradictions inherent in their efforts.

Limitations of Diaspora Engagement in Socio-Political Reforms

(i) Disconnect from Local Realities

One of the most significant challenges faced by the Punjabi diaspora is their potential disconnect from the ground realities of Punjab. Many diaspora members, particularly those born and raised abroad, may lack a nuanced understanding of the socio-political, economic, and cultural dynamics of their ancestral homeland. This disconnect can lead to well-intentioned but misaligned initiatives that fail to address the root causes of local issues.

For example, diaspora-funded projects in education or healthcare may prioritize infrastructure development without considering the systemic barriers, such as corruption, bureaucratic inefficiency, or social inequalities, that hinder the effective implementation of these projects. This misalignment can result in wasted resources and unmet expectations, undermining the diaspora's credibility and impact.

From a sociological perspective, this challenge reflects the limitations of transnationalism, where physical and cultural distance can create gaps in knowledge and understanding. While the diaspora's global perspective is valuable, it must be complemented by a deep engagement with local contexts to ensure that their interventions are relevant and effective.

(ii) Power Dynamics and Elite Capture

Another critical limitation is the power dynamics between the diaspora and local communities. Diaspora members often bring financial resources, expertise, and global networks, which can position them as dominant actors in development initiatives. This power imbalance can lead to a form of "elite capture", where local elites or intermediaries co-opt diaspora resources for their own benefit, rather than for the collective good of the community.

For instance, diaspora-funded projects may be influenced by local political or economic interests, diverting resources away from marginalized groups and reinforcing existing inequalities. This dynamic can create tensions between the diaspora and local communities, eroding trust and undermining the sustainability of development efforts.

From a sociological perspective, this issue can be analysed through the lens of power and inequality, where the distribution of resources and decision-making authority shapes the outcomes of development initiatives. Addressing this challenge requires a more participatory approach, where local communities are actively involved in the planning and implementation of diaspora-led projects.

(iii) Cultural Hybridity and Identity Conflicts

The cultural hybridity of the Punjabi diaspora, while a source of strength, can also create identity conflicts that complicate their engagement in socio-political reforms. Second and third-generation Punjabis often navigate dual identities, balancing their Punjabi heritage with the cultural norms of their host countries. This hybridity can lead to misunderstandings or conflicts with local communities, particularly when diaspora members are perceived as imposing foreign values or practices.

For example, diaspora-led initiatives that promote gender equality or secular education may clash with traditional norms and values in Punjab, leading to resistance from local communities. These conflicts can hinder the effectiveness of diaspora interventions and create tensions that undermine their legitimacy.

From a sociological perspective, this challenge reflects the complexities of cultural hybridity, where the negotiation of identity is an ongoing and contested process. To navigate these conflicts, the diaspora must adopt a culturally sensitive approach that respects local traditions while advocating for progressive change.

(iv) Sustainability and Dependency

A common criticism of diaspora-led development initiatives is their lack of sustainability. Many projects rely heavily on external funding and expertise, creating a dependency that can undermine local capacity and ownership. When diaspora members withdraw their support, either due to shifting priorities or resource constraints, these projects often struggle to sustain their impact.

For instance, diaspora-funded schools or healthcare facilities may face challenges in maintaining their operations once external funding is no longer available. This dependency can create a cycle of short-term interventions that fail to address the structural causes of poverty and inequality.

From a sociological perspective, this issue highlights the importance of building local capacity and fostering community ownership in development initiatives. Sustainable change requires a shift from external dependency to internal empowerment, where local communities are equipped with the skills and resources to drive their own development.

(v) Political Instrumentalization and Backlash

The socio-political engagement of the Punjabi diaspora can also be subject to political instrumentalization, where their efforts are co-opted or manipulated by political actors for their own agendas. This instrumentalization can lead to a backlash against the diaspora, particularly when their interventions are perceived as interfering in local politics or undermining national sovereignty.

For example, diaspora advocacy for human rights or environmental reforms may be framed as foreign interference by political elites seeking to maintain their power. This backlash can create a hostile environment for diaspora engagement, limiting their ability to effect meaningful change.

From a sociological perspective, this challenge reflects the contested nature of transnationalism, where the boundaries between local and global actors are constantly negotiated. To navigate this complexity, the diaspora must adopt a collaborative and non-partisan approach that prioritizes the interests of local communities over political agendas.

Impact on Nation-Building

The challenges and criticisms faced by the Punjabi diaspora in their socio-political engagement have significant implications for nation-building in contemporary contexts. While their contributions are valuable, the limitations of their engagement highlight the need for a more nuanced and context-sensitive approach to development. By addressing these challenges, the diaspora can enhance their impact and contribute to the creation of a more inclusive and equitable society in Punjab.

In today's globalized world, the role of younger generations in nation-building is deeply intertwined with its ability to navigate the complexities of transnationalism and cultural hybridity. By leveraging their education, expertise, and networks, they can create a sense of unity and purpose that transcends national borders. However, this requires a commitment to understanding local contexts, fostering community ownership, and addressing power dynamics that shape the outcomes of their efforts.

The challenges and criticisms faced by the Punjabi diaspora in their socio-political engagement highlight the complexities of transnationalism and the need for a more nuanced approach to development. By addressing these limitations, the diaspora can enhance their impact and contribute to the creation of a more inclusive and equitable society in Punjab. Their efforts reflect the interconnectedness of global and local identities in a rapidly changing world, shaping the future of nation-building in the 21st century.

7

Intergenerational Dynamics and Cultural Heritage

7.1 Cultural Preservation across Generations

The preservation of cultural heritage across generations is a complex and dynamic process, particularly for diasporic communities such as second and third-generation Punjabis. These generations play a pivotal role in maintaining the cultural traditions, values, and practices of their ancestors while navigating the challenges of cultural assimilation and identity crises in multicultural societies. From a sociological perspective, this process is deeply intertwined with theories of cultural transmission, identity formation, and the negotiation of hybrid identities in a globalized world.

- **Role of Second and Third-Generation Punjabis in Maintaining Cultural Heritage**

Second and third-generation Punjabis, born and raised in diasporic contexts, often find themselves at the intersection of multiple cultural worlds. They are tasked with the responsibility of preserving their ancestral heritage while adopting to the dominant cultural norms of their host societies. This dual role is both a privilege and a burden, as it requires a delicate balance between tradition and modernity.

1. *Cultural Transmission and Socialization*

Cultural preservation begins within the family unit, where parents and elders serve as the primary agents of cultural transmission. For Punjabis, this often involves teaching children the Punjabi language, religious practices, and traditional customs such as festivals (e.g., *Vaisakhi, Lohri*), music (e.g., *Bhangra, Giddha*), and cuisine. However, the effectiveness of this transmission is influenced by the degree of cultural immersion in the host society. Second and third-generation Punjabis often experience a dilution of cultural practices as they are exposed to and influenced by the dominant culture.

According to Berry's (1997) acculturation model, individuals in diasporic communities adopt different strategies to navigate their cultural identity, including assimilation, separation, integration, and marginalization. Second and third-generation Punjabis often lean toward integration, where they selectively adopt aspects of both their heritage and host cultures. This selective adoption allows them to maintain a connection to their roots while functioning effectively in their societal context.

2. *Institutional Support for Cultural Preservation*

Beyond the family, institutional structures such as religious organizations (e.g., *gurdwaras*), community centres, and cultural associations play a crucial role in preserving Punjabi heritage. These institutions provide spaces for communal gatherings, religious education, and cultural celebrations, fostering a sense of belonging and continuity. For instance, *gurdwaras* often serve as hubs for teaching Punjabi language classes, organizing youth camps, and hosting religious festivals, ensuring that younger generations remain connected to their cultural roots.

However, the effectiveness of these institutions is often limited by generational differences. While first-generation immigrants may prioritize traditional practices, second and third-generation Punjabis may seek to modernize or reinterpret these practices to align with their contemporary realities. This tension between tradition and modernity can lead to conflicts within the community, but also opens avenues for innovative forms of cultural expression.

3. *Cultural Hybridity and Innovation*

Second and third-generation Punjabis often engage in cultural hybridity, blending elements of their heritage with contemporary global influences. This is evident in the evolution of Punjabi music, fashion, and art. For example, the global popularity of *Bhangra* music, which has been fused with hip-hop, electronic, and pop genres, demonstrates how younger generations are redefining Punjabi culture for a global audience.

Cultural hybridity also extends to language use, where younger Punjabis may code-switch between Punjabi and English, creating a unique linguistic identity. While this hybridity is often viewed as a sign of cultural erosion, it can also be seen as a form of cultural resilience, as it allows Punjabi heritage to remain relevant in a rapidly changing world.

• Challenges of Cultural Assimilation and Identity Crisis

Despite their efforts to preserve their cultural heritage, second and third-generation Punjabis face significant challenges related to cultural assimilation and identity formation. These challenges are shaped by broader societal forces, including globalization, racism, and the pressure to conform to dominant cultural norms.

1. *Cultural Assimilation and Erosion*

Cultural assimilation refers to the process by which individuals or groups adopt the cultural traits of another group, often at the expense of their own heritage. For second and third-generation Punjabis, assimilation is often driven by the desire to fit into the dominant culture and avoid marginalization. This can lead to the erosion of cultural practices, particularly those that are perceived as incompatible with the values of the host society.

For example, the Punjabi language is often one of the first casualties of cultural assimilation. Many second and third-generation Punjabis grow up speaking English as their primary language, with limited proficiency in Punjabi. This linguistic shift not only hinders communication with older generations but also weakens their connection to Punjabi literature, poetry, and oral traditions.

The pressure to assimilate is further compounded by systemic racism and discrimination, which can lead to internalized shame or rejection of one's cultural heritage. This is particularly evident in societies where minority cultures are stigmatized or exoticized, leading to a sense of cultural inferiority among younger generations.

2. *Identity Crisis and Dual Belonging*

The experience of dual belonging being simultaneously connected to one's heritage culture and the dominant culture can lead to identity crises among second and third-generation Punjabis. This is especially true in societies where multiculturalism is superficially celebrated but structurally undermined. Younger Punjabis may struggle to reconcile their Punjabi identity with their national identity, leading to feelings of alienation and fragmentation.

Hall's (1990) concept of "cultural identity" highlights the fluid and contested nature of identity formation in diasporic communities. For second and third-generation Punjabis, cultural identity is not a fixed or monolithic construct but a dynamic process of negotiation and redefinition. This process is often fraught with tension, as they navigate conflicting expectations from their families, communities, and broader society.

3. *Generational Conflicts and Cultural Gaps*

Generational conflicts are a common feature of diasporic communities, as younger generations often challenge the cultural norms and values of their elders. These conflicts can manifest in various ways, from disagreements over marriage practices (e.g., arranged marriages *vs.* love marriages) to differing attitudes toward gender roles and religious observance.

For instance, second and third-generation Punjabi women may resist traditional gender roles that prioritize domesticity and subservience, seeking instead to assert their independence and pursue careers. While this represents a positive shift toward gender equality, it can also create friction within families and communities, as older generations may view these changes as a threat to cultural continuity.

4. *The Role of Media and Technology*

Media and technology play a dual role in shaping the cultural experiences of second and third-generation Punjabis. On the one hand, digital platforms provide access to Punjabi music, films, and literature, enabling younger generations to engage with their heritage in new and meaningful ways. On the other hand, the pervasive influence of global media can accelerate cultural assimilation by promoting dominant cultural norms and values.

Social media, in particular, has become a powerful tool for cultural expression and activism among younger Punjabis. Platforms like Instagram, YouTube, and TikTok allow them to share their experiences, challenge stereotypes, and connect with other members of the diaspora. However, these platforms can also perpetuate cultural commodification and superficial representations of Punjabi culture, reducing it to a set of exoticized symbols and practices.

5. *The Role of Intergenerational Cultural Conservation towards Nation-Building in Modern Societies*

Intergenerational conservation of cultural heritage, especially in the case of diasporic communities such as second and third-generation Punjabis, carries deep implications for nation-building in the modern globalized world. Nation-building is the act of building or organizing a national identity through the authority of the state, and it usually includes creating a feeling of unity, common values, and common purpose among different populations. In multicultural societies, intergenerational cultural preservation plays a vital role in shaping cohesive and inclusive national identities. This part discusses how the second and third-generation Punjabis' attempts to preserve their cultural identity influence nation-building, with themes revolving around multiculturalism, social cohesion, and the negotiation of hybrid identities.

• The Impact of Intergenerational Cultural Preservation on Nation-Building in Contemporary Societies

The preservation of cultural heritage across generations, particularly among diasporic communities like second and third-generation Punjabis, plays a significant role in nation-building in today's globalized world. Nation-building, which involves constructing a shared national identity, relies on fostering unity, shared values, and collective purpose among diverse populations. In multicultural societies such as Canada, the UK, and Australia, where large Punjabi communities reside, the efforts of younger generations to maintain their cultural heritage enrich the national cultural fabric and promote inclusivity. Through their contributions to arts, music, cuisine, and religious practices, second and third-generation Punjabis introduce elements of Punjabi culture into the mainstream, challenging monolithic notions of national identity and fostering a pluralistic vision of nationhood. However, this process is not without challenges, as cultural preservation can sometimes be met with resistance from segments of the dominant population who view diversity as a threat to national unity. Issues such as racism, discrimination, and cultural marginalization can hinder the full participation of these communities in nation-building, necessitating policies that promote anti-racism, equity, and cultural rights.

Social cohesion, a key component of nation-building, is strengthened by the intergenerational transmission of cultural heritage, which fosters a sense of belonging and continuity within communities. Younger Punjabis often bridge generational divides by adopting traditional practices to contemporary contexts, such as celebrating festivals like *Vaisakhi* and *Lohri* with both traditional and modern elements. These efforts not only strengthen community bonds but also promote intercultural dialogue and understanding, contributing to a broader sense of solidarity. However, tensions can arise when cultural preservation is perceived as separatism or resistance to integration, such as in the establishment of ethnic enclaves or the prioritization of heritage languages over the national language. To address these challenges, a balanced approach to nation-building is essential, one that values both diversity and unity through policies supporting bilingual education, intercultural exchange, and community engagement.

The concept of hybrid identities, where second and third-generation Punjabis blend elements of their heritage culture with global and local influences, is central to redefining nationhood in more inclusive and dynamic terms. This hybridity serves as a source of cultural innovation, as seen in the fusion of *Bhangra* music with hip-hop or electronic genres, which revitalizes traditional *Punjabi* culture while making it accessible to a wider audience. Such innovations enrich national identity by incorporating diverse perspectives and challenging static or homogeneous notions of culture. Additionally, the transnational dimension of hybrid identities reflects the realities of a globalized world, where cultural boundaries are increasingly porous. For younger Punjabis, national identity extends beyond the borders of their host country to include transnational networks connecting them to their ancestral homeland and other diasporic communities. This interconnectedness highlights the need for nations to adopt a more global perspective in their nation-building efforts, recognizing the hybrid identities of their diverse populations as a source of strength. By embracing these complexities, nations can build more inclusive and resilient national identities that reflect the realities of the 21st century.

7.2 Contributions to Nation-Building

The contributions of diasporic communities, particularly second and third-generation Punjabis, to nation-building are multifaceted and deeply rooted in their intergenerational dynamics. These contributions manifest in various forms, including philanthropic and entrepreneurial activities, as well as strategies for maintaining connections with their ancestral homeland, Punjab. From a sociological perspective, these efforts reflect broader themes of transnationalism, cultural hybridity, and the negotiation of identity in a globalized world. This section delves into the intergenerational differences in philanthropic and entrepreneurial activities among Punjabis and explores the strategies they employ to maintain connections with

Punjab, highlighting their implications for nation-building in contemporary societies.

• Intergenerational Differences in Philanthropic and Entrepreneurial Activities

Philanthropy and entrepreneurship are two key avenues through which second and third-generation Punjabis contribute to nation-building in both their host countries and their ancestral homeland. However, the approaches and motivations behind these activities often differ across generations, reflecting shifts in cultural values, economic opportunities, and global connectivity.

1. *Philanthropic Activities: Generational Shifts in Priorities*

First-generation Punjabi immigrants often engage in philanthropy as a way to give back to their communities and maintain ties with their cultural roots. Their philanthropic efforts are typically directed toward religious institutions, such as *gurdwaras*, and community organizations that support newly arrived immigrants. These activities are deeply rooted in the Sikh principle of *seva* (selfless service), which emphasizes the importance of contributing to the welfare of others.

In contrast, second and third-generation Punjabis tend to adopt a more global and secular approach to philanthropy. While they may still support religious and cultural institutions, their philanthropic activities often extend to broader social causes, such as education, healthcare, and environmental sustainability. This shift reflects their integration into the societal norms of their host countries, where philanthropy is often framed in terms of social responsibility and civic engagement.

For example, many second and third-generation Punjabis in countries like Canada and the United States have established foundations and non-profit organizations that address issues such as poverty alleviation, gender equality, and youth empowerment.

These initiatives not only contribute to the development of their host countries but also strengthen their connection to global humanitarian efforts.

From a sociological perspective, this generational shift in philanthropic priorities can be understood through the lens of acculturation and identity negotiation. As younger Punjabis navigate their dual identities, they seek to balance their cultural heritage with the values of their host societies, resulting in a more inclusive and globally oriented approach to philanthropy.

2. *Entrepreneurial Activities: Innovation and Economic Contributions*

Entrepreneurship is another significant avenue through which Punjabis contribute to nation-building. First-generation Punjabi immigrants often establish small businesses, such as grocery stores, restaurants, and transportation services, as a means of economic survival and upward mobility. These businesses not only provide livelihoods for their families but also contribute to the local economies of their host countries.

Second and third-generation Punjabis, on the other hand, are more likely to pursue entrepreneurship in innovative and technology-driven sectors. This shift reflects their higher levels of education, access to capital, and exposure to global markets. For example, many younger Punjabis have founded start-ups in fields such as information technology, healthcare, and renewable energy, contributing to the economic growth and technological advancement of their host countries.

The entrepreneurial activities of younger Punjabis also have a transnational dimension, as they often leverage their connections to Punjab and other parts of the global Punjabi diaspora. For instance, some entrepreneurs have established businesses that facilitate trade and investment between their host countries and Punjab, creating economic opportunities on both sides.

From a sociological perspective, the entrepreneurial activities of second and third-generation Punjabis can be analysed through the framework of transnationalism, which emphasizes the interconnectedness of diasporic communities across national borders. By engaging in transnational entrepreneurship, younger Punjabis contribute to the economic development of both their host countries and their ancestral homeland, thereby playing a dual role in nation-building.

• Strategies for Maintaining Connections with Punjab

Maintaining connections with Punjab is a central aspect of the cultural identity of second and third-generation Punjabis. These connections are sustained through various strategies, including visits to Punjab, participation in cultural and religious events, and the use of digital technologies. These strategies not only reinforce their cultural heritage but also contribute to the socio-economic development of Punjab, thereby impacting nation-building in both their host countries and India.

1. *Visits to Punjab: Cultural Reconnection and Economic Impact*

Regular visits to Punjab are a common strategy employed by second and third-generation Punjabis to maintain their cultural and familial ties. These visits often coincide with major festivals, such as *Vaisakhi* and *Diwali*, or family events, such as weddings and religious ceremonies. For younger Punjabis, these trips serve as an opportunity to reconnect with their roots, learn about their cultural heritage, and strengthen their sense of identity.

From a sociological perspective, these visits can be understood as a form of cultural pilgrimage, where individuals seek to reaffirm their connection to their ancestral homeland. This process is particularly important for younger generations, who may feel disconnected from their cultural heritage due to the pressures of assimilation and globalization.

In addition to their cultural significance, visits to Punjab also have an economic impact. The influx of remittances and spending by diasporic Punjabis contributes to the local economy, supporting businesses such as hotels, restaurants, and transportation services. Furthermore, some second and third-generation Punjabis invest in real estate, agriculture, or small businesses in Punjab, creating employment opportunities and fostering economic development.

2. Participation in Cultural and Religious Events

Participation in cultural and religious events is another key strategy for maintaining connections with Punjab. These events, which are often organized by Punjabi community organizations and religious institutions, provide a space for younger generations to engage with their cultural heritage and build a sense of community.

For example, events such as *Bhangra* competitions, Punjabi language classes, and Sikh youth camps are popular among second and third-generation Punjabis. These activities not only promote cultural preservation but also foster intergenerational solidarity by bringing together older and younger members of the community.

From a sociological perspective, these events serve as sites of cultural reproduction, where traditional practices and values are transmitted to younger generations. At the same time, they also provide opportunities for cultural innovation, as younger Punjabis reinterpret and adopt these practices to reflect their contemporary realities.

3. *Use of Digital Technologies: Virtual Connections and Transnational Networks*

The use of digital technologies has revolutionized the way

second and third-generation Punjabis maintain connections with Punjab. Social media platforms, such as Facebook, Instagram, and WhatsApp, enable them to stay connected with family and friends in Punjab, participate in cultural and religious events, and access Punjabi media content.

Digital technologies also facilitate transnational networks that connect Punjabi diasporic communities across the globe. For example, online forums and social media groups provide a platform for Punjabis to share information, exchange ideas, and collaborate on projects related to cultural preservation and community development.

From a sociological perspective, the use of digital technologies can be analysed through the framework of transnationalism and virtual communities. These technologies enable younger Punjabis to maintain a sense of belonging to their ancestral homeland while also participating in the cultural and economic life of their host countries. This dual engagement contributes to the development of hybrid identities that are both locally rooted and globally connected.

7.4 Impact on Punjab's Global Identity

The global identity of Punjab, a region with a rich cultural heritage and a vibrant diaspora, has been significantly shaped by the efforts of younger generations, particularly second and third-generation Punjabis. These individuals, born and raised in diasporic contexts, play a crucial role in promoting Punjabi culture on a global scale. Through their engagement with arts, music, language, and digital media, they not only preserve their cultural heritage but also redefine it in ways that resonate with contemporary global audiences. From a sociological perspective, this process reflects broader themes of cultural hybridity, transnationalism, and the negotiation of identity in a globalized world.

• Role of Younger Generations in Promoting Punjabi Culture Globally

1. *Cultural Hybridity and Innovation*

Second and third-generation Punjabis are at the forefront of cultural hybridity, blending traditional Punjabi elements with global influences to create innovative forms of cultural expression. This is particularly evident in the realm of music, where genres like *Bhangra* have been fused with hip-hop, electronic, and pop music to create a unique sound that appeals to diverse audiences. Artists such as Jazzy B., Diljit Dosanjh, and Sidhu Moosewala have gained international recognition, bringing Punjabi music to global stages and streaming platforms.

This cultural innovation is not limited to music. Younger Punjabis are also redefining Punjabi fashion, cuisine, and art, making them accessible and appealing to a wider audience. For example, the popularity of Punjabi street food, such as butter chicken and *chole bhature*, has transcended cultural boundaries, becoming a staple in global culinary scenes. Similarly, Punjabi-inspired fashion, characterized by vibrant colours and intricate embroidery, has influenced global fashion trends.

From a sociological perspective, this process of cultural hybridity can be understood through Appadurai's (1996) concept of global cultural flows, which emphasizes the interconnectedness of cultural practices in a globalized world. By blending traditional and modern elements, younger Punjabis create a dynamic and evolving cultural identity that reflects their dual belonging to both their heritage and host cultures.

2. *Digital Media and Transnational Networks*

The advent of digital media has revolutionized the way Punjabi culture is promoted and consumed globally. Social media platforms, such as YouTube, Instagram, and TikTok, have become powerful tools for younger Punjabis to share their cultural heritage with a global audience. These platforms enable them to create and disseminate content that showcases Punjabi music, dance, language, and traditions, reaching millions of viewers worldwide.

For example, Punjabi-language YouTube channels and Instagram influencers have gained massive followings, providing a platform for cultural expression and exchange. These digital spaces not only promote Punjabi culture but also foster a sense of community among diasporic Punjabis, creating transnational networks that transcend geographical boundaries.

From a sociological perspective, the use of digital media can be analysed through the framework of virtual communities and transnationalism. These technologies enable younger Punjabis to maintain a connection to their cultural roots while also engaging with global audiences, thereby contributing to the globalization of Punjabi culture.

3. *Language Preservation and Promotion*

Language is a key component of cultural identity, and younger Punjabis play a vital role in preserving and promoting the Punjabi language globally. Despite the challenges of cultural assimilation, many second and third-generation Punjabis are making concerted efforts to learn and speak Punjabi, often through formal education, community programmes, and digital resources.

The promotion of the Punjabi language is also evident in the global success of Punjabi-language films, music, and literature. Punjabi cinema, often referred to as Pollywood, has gained international recognition, with films like *Jatt & Juliet* and *Sardaar Ji* attracting audiences beyond the Punjabi diaspora. Similarly, Punjabi literature and poetry are being translated and shared globally, highlighting the richness of the language and its cultural significance.

From a sociological perspective, the preservation and promotion of the Punjabi language can be understood through Bourdieu's (1986) concept of cultural capital. Language serves as a form of cultural capital that is essential for maintaining cultural identity and transmitting it to future generations. By promoting the Punjabi language, younger Punjabis contribute to the preservation of their cultural heritage and its global recognition.

4. *Cultural Diplomacy and Soft Power*

The efforts of younger Punjabis to promote their culture globally also have implications for cultural diplomacy and soft power. By showcasing Punjabi culture on international platforms, they enhance the global image of Punjab and contribute to the cultural diplomacy of India. This is particularly important in a globalized world, where cultural exchange and soft power play a crucial role in shaping international relations.

For example, the global popularity of Punjabi music and cinema has not only brought recognition to Punjabi culture but also fostered a sense of pride and identity among the Punjabi diaspora. This cultural diplomacy creates a positive image of Punjab and India, contributing to the nation's soft power and global influence.

From a sociological perspective, this process can be analysed through the lens of cultural globalization and soft power theory. By promoting their culture globally, younger Punjabis contribute to the cultural globalization of Punjab and enhance its soft power, thereby shaping its global identity.

Impact on Nation-Building

The contributions of second and third-generation Punjabis to nation-building are significant and multifaceted. Their philanthropic and entrepreneurial activities not only contribute to the economic and social development of their host countries but also strengthen their connection to Punjab, creating a transnational network of cultural and economic exchange. These efforts reflect the broader themes of multiculturalism, social cohesion, and hybrid identities, which are central to the process of nation-building in contemporary societies.

For example, the philanthropic initiatives of younger Punjabis address pressing social issues in their host countries, such as education and healthcare, while also supporting development projects in Punjab. Similarly, their entrepreneurial activities contribute to the economic growth of their host countries and create opportunities for trade and investment in Punjab. These dual contributions highlight the interconnectedness of diasporic communities and their role in fostering global citizenship.

At the same time, the strategies employed by second and third-generation Punjabis to maintain connections with Punjab reinforce their cultural identity and promote intergenerational solidarity. By participating in cultural and religious events, visiting Punjab, and using digital technologies, they create a sense of continuity and belonging that transcends national borders. This transnational dimension of their identity challenges traditional notions of nationhood and contributes to the development of more inclusive and dynamic national identities.

The role of younger generations in promoting Punjabi culture globally is a testament to their resilience, creativity, and commitment to preserving their cultural heritage. Through cultural hybridity, digital media, language preservation, and cultural diplomacy, they have redefined Punjab's global identity, making it a vibrant and dynamic force in the global cultural landscape. Their efforts not only enrich the cultural fabric of their host countries but also contribute to the global recognition and appreciation of Punjabi culture, highlighting the interconnectedness of cultural identities in a globalized world.

In today's context, the contributions of younger generations to nation-building are deeply intertwined with their efforts to promote and preserve their cultural heritage. By engaging in cultural diplomacy, fostering transnational networks, and innovating traditional practices, they create a sense of unity and pride that transcends national borders. These efforts reflect the complexities of living in a globalized world, where cultural identities are constantly negotiated and redefined. By embracing these complexities, younger generations contribute to the development of more inclusive and resilient national identities, shaping the future of nation-building in the 21st century.

8

Transnational Networks and Socio-economic Development

8.1 Role of Remittances and Investments

The Punjabi diaspora has long been a significant driver of socio-economic development in Punjab, primarily through remittances and investments. These financial flows, facilitated by transnational networks, have had a profound impact on Punjab's economy, infrastructure, and social fabric. From a sociological perspective, the role of remittances and investments can be understood through frameworks such as transnationalism, social capital, and global economic integration. This section explores the economic impact of remittances on Punjab's development and examines diaspora-led entrepreneurial ventures, highlighting their contributions to nation-building in contemporary contexts.

Punjab's socio-economic development by the Punjabi diaspora is best seen by way of remittances and investments by the diaspora that have altered rural as well as urban environments in Punjab. Remittances from states such as the UK, Canada, the US, and Australia, over several decades, have been a much-needed financial survival tool for scores of families within Punjab. Household consumption, schooling, medical costs, marriage charges, and even the construction of land or homes benefit from these remittances. Villages within Doaba districts, particularly Jalandhar, Hoshiarpur, and Nawanshahr, are dramatic examples of the ways in which transnational financial flows reconstitute local economies and social hierarchies. Transnational networks do not just allow money to flow, but also ideas, aspirations, and practices, including lifestyle, consumption patterns, and political affiliations, to shape Punjab. Sociologically, these networks encapsulate what Peggy Levitt (2001) refers to as "social remittances", the diffusion of values, norms, and practices, which can cause positive and unforeseen alterations in the home society.

Diaspora-initiated entrepreneurial enterprises also carry forward the development influence of the Punjabi diaspora. Successful diasporic entrepreneurs usually return to Punjab or invest in education, healthcare, hospitality, and agro-industries. For example, overseas donor-named schools and colleges have become commonplace in the Doaba region, symbolizing a wish among the diaspora to contribute to their communities while at the same time accruing symbolic capital. These investments have generated jobs, enhanced access to services, and brought professional practices influenced by international standards. Additionally, philanthropic activities like sponsoring *gurdwaras*, community centres, and disaster relief programmes indicate a changing perception of shared responsibility and emotional connection with the homeland. As the diaspora engages actively in a nation-building process beyond borders, they contribute not only financially but culturally and ideologically to the concept of Punjab and India as globalized yet grounded societies.

At the same time, it is also important to realize that the development effect of such financial flows is not uniformly shared. Remittances are most likely to advantage middle- and upper-caste households with networks established overseas, while numerous disadvantaged households continue to be left behind. Moreover, the emphasis on conspicuous consumption in the form of high-end housing and overseas schooling at times ignores the imperative for sustainable, equitable development. Thus, as much as the financial and social capital of the Punjabi diaspora does undoubtedly contribute to nation-building, the contribution must be critically examined. Development policies must focus on directing remittances into productive sectors, including local entrepreneurship, renewable energy, and rural infrastructure, to create broad-based benefits. Fostering participatory models of development wherein diaspora members co-operate with local governance institutions and civil society can produce more equitable outcomes. Eventually, the Punjabi diaspora's contribution to nation-building is not only in remitting capital but in how they approach issues of equity, sustainability, and overall transformation of the homeland.

Economic Impact of Remittances on Punjab's Development

1. *Remittances as a Catalyst for Economic Growth*

Remittances (money sent by migrants to their families back home) are a vital source of income for many households in Punjab. According to the World Bank, India is the largest recipient of remittances globally, with Punjab being one of the top beneficiary states. These funds are often used to meet basic needs, such as food, housing, and healthcare, thereby improving the standard of living for recipient families.

Beyond household consumption, remittances also contribute to local economic growth by increasing disposable income and stimulating demand for goods and services. For example, the influx of remittances has led to the growth of small businesses, such as retail shops, restaurants, and transportation services, creating employment opportunities and boosting the local economy.

From a sociological perspective, remittances can be seen as a form of social capital, where financial resources are transferred through familial and community networks. These networks not only facilitate the flow of money but also strengthen social ties between the diaspora and their ancestral homeland, fostering a sense of collective responsibility and solidarity.

Remittances from the Punjabi diaspora form a key pillar of the economic and social growth of Punjab, and they serve not only as the lifeline for many families but also as a determinant force in driving overall regional development. For thousands of families, the remittances fill the gap between poverty and economic stability, allowing them access to basic services like healthcare, education, and shelter that would otherwise be out of reach. Entire villages in Malwa and the Doaba belt, which have high rates of international migration, have seen visible change because of the remittance-boosted wealth. Good buildings, upmarket amenities, and better infrastructure are all material pointers to this finance-driven change caused by transnational flows. The consistent flow of funds from nations such as Canada, the United Kingdom, and Australia provides a constant flow of capital into rural economies, supporting consumer spending by households and enhancing general living standards.

Remittances are important in that they not only satisfy private demands, but also spur public and semi-public goods. Enhanced purchasing power in remittance-recipient households generates demand for goods and services, which in turn expands local markets and entrepreneurship. This has promoted the development of micro-enterprises like neighbourhood transport firms, tailoring outfits, coaching schools, and travelling repair shops in most regions. The resulting jobs counteract underemployment, and rural distress migration and help create a diversified rural economy. Additionally, the multiplier impact of remittance expenditure more consumption stimulates output and services adds to the general dynamism of local economies.

From a sociological perspective, remittances are more than economic capital; they are embedded in networks of cultural obligation, reciprocity, and trust. Such transnational flows support kinship relationships, underwrite cultural festivals, and allow diaspora members to engage actively in their communities even though they are physically remote. This socio-cultural embeddedness commonly takes the form of diaspora-initiated philanthropic efforts like sponsoring schools in villages, holding medical camps, or restoring community centres that fuel grassroots development and enhance the region's social fabric. Such acts of giving are not just enactments of family duty but also strong articulations of transnational belonging and identity.

In the larger nation-building discourse, remittances by the Punjabi diaspora are an informal, decentralized development financing that supplements state-led formal processes. Their contributions, varying from the well-being of individual households to community development, are essential in compensating for structural gaps in rural governance and public service delivery. The reliance on remittances needs to be subject to critical scrutiny as well. The wealth generated through remittances can give rise to socio-economic differences between the migrant and the non-migrant households, resulting in caste and class differentiation. In addition to this, increasing the practice of investing in unproductive assets, like property, luxury cars, and pompous ceremonies, will lead to distorting a pattern of development oriented towards consumption as opposed to durable growth.

In order to leverage the maximum potential of remittances for nation-building, policy-makers need to bring in inclusive financial instruments that invest these funds in productive sectors such as renewable energy, agrotech, skill development, and education. Government programmes like the Pravasi Kaushal Vikas Yojana (PKVY) and the India Development Foundation of Overseas Indians (IDF-OI) can be reinforced to offer platforms for diaspora investment in infrastructure and social entrepreneurship. Diaspora bonds and community-based remittance pooling schemes may also be considered as new financial instruments. Finally, a well-coordinated framework that connects diaspora dreams with local development agendas can turn remittances into sustainable drivers of change, making meaningful contributions not only to Punjab's prosperity, but to India's inclusive and participatory nation-building process as a whole.

2. *Impact on Education and Human Capital Development*

One of the most significant impacts of remittances is their contribution to education and human capital development. Many families in Punjab use remittances to fund their children's education, enabling them to attend better schools, pursue higher education, and acquire skills that enhance their employability. This investment in education has long-term benefits, as it equips individuals with the knowledge and skills needed to participate in the global economy.

For instance, remittance-funded education has enabled many young Punjabis to secure jobs in sectors such as information technology, healthcare, and engineering, both within India and abroad. This not only improves their economic prospects but also contributes to the development of Punjab by creating a skilled workforce that can drive innovation and productivity.

From a sociological perspective, this emphasis on education reflects the diaspora's commitment to human capital development, which is essential for breaking the cycle of poverty and inequality. By investing in education, the diaspora empowers individuals and communities to challenge systemic barriers and advocate for their rights, thereby contributing to the democratization of society.

The Punjabi diaspora's investment in education in the form of remittances has become a revolutionary force for changing the socio-economic fabric of Punjab. The financial inputs make it possible for families to provide private education, coaching for entrance exams, and higher education a possibility that otherwise may not be available, particularly in rural and underprivileged communities. Education as a means for upward mobility is facilitated, and remittance-sustained families tend to spearhead new possibilities for academic and professional achievement. This increased level of education spurs migration ambitions in the younger generation, creating a virtuous circle of migration and education, encouraging, further migration or skilled work.

Even more significantly, this educational progress directly adds to human capital development in Punjab. Graduates equipped with diaspora-sponsored training tend to go on to enter technical professions demanding technical skills and global awareness, raising economic competitiveness in the region. Their entry into sectors such as IT, finance, and healthcare not only increases personal earnings but also reinforces the service and knowledge economies of Punjab. In addition, most of them ultimately return or interact with their original communities, transferring skills, generating jobs, or mentoring young people in the community thereby enhancing the effects of education investment.

From a sociological view point, this focus on human capital formation is consistent with a vision of participatory nation-building on a larger scale. The diaspora's focus on education undermines entrenched inequalities by empowering marginalized groups to gain access to new social and economic opportunities. It also creates a culture of meritocracy and self-improvement, in which success is associated with learning, not birth. These changes are necessary for building a more inclusive and dynamic society. In order to further capitalize on this potential, the state can partner with diaspora networks to create scholarship funds, skill development centres, and online learning platforms, institutionalizing diaspora support for human capital development and integrating it deeper into India's nation-building agenda.

3. *Challenges and Limitations of Remittances*

While remittances have a positive impact on Punjab's economy, they also have limitations that need to be addressed. One major challenge is the dependency on remittances, which can create a culture of complacency and discourage local entrepreneurship. In some cases, families may rely solely on remittances for their livelihood, rather than seeking opportunities for economic self-sufficiency.

Additionally, the uneven distribution of remittances can exacerbate existing inequalities, as wealthier households are more likely to receive larger amounts of money. This can create disparities in access to education, healthcare, and other resources, further marginalizing vulnerable groups.

From a sociological perspective, these challenges highlight the need for a more balanced approach to development, where remittances are complemented by policies that promote local entrepreneurship, job creation, and social equity.

Although remittances have undoubtedly altered the economic face of Punjab and helped individual prosperity, their long-term developmental influence is not without constraints. Over-reliance on remittances can create economic stagnation at the grassroots level, were recipients, particularly in rural communities, might spend more on consumption rather than investing in productive assets or enterprise. Such fiscal dependence may curb entrepreneurial energy and entrepreneurship, breeding an environment in which economic support from overseas is regarded as the central mechanism for sustenance as opposed to complementing home-grown economic activity. This reliance in the long term might lead young people to eschew participation in agriculture, domestic industry, or state efforts to stimulate independence and job growth.

Furthermore, the disparate access to opportunities for migration sometimes intermediated by class, kinship groups, and education levels guarantees that remittances are not uniformly allocated. The better-off households, capable of incurring the costs of emigration, capture larger portions of remittance inflows. This entrenches rural inequalities and locks in economic gains within a small fraction of society, intensifying the same disparities development purports to solve. From a sociological perspective, such disparities serve as a reminder that remittances by themselves cannot propel comprehensive development or social justice.

In nation-building, it becomes imperative to direct diaspora involvement in a manner that benefits the larger society. Policies need to encourage inclusive financial education, encourage diaspora-led investments in backward areas, and foster collaboration between return migrants and local entrepreneurs. Government and civil society need to work together to construct systems in which remittances function as seed capital, not safety nets driving innovation, diversifying livelihoods, and making the benefits of transnational linkages are felt more evenly across all segments of Punjabi society.

Diaspora-led Entrepreneurial Ventures in Punjab

1. *Entrepreneurship as a Driver of Economic Development*

In addition to remittances, the Punjabi diaspora has played a crucial role in driving economic development through entrepreneurial ventures. Many diaspora members have established businesses in Punjab, ranging from small-scale enterprises to large-scale industries, creating jobs and stimulating economic growth.

For example, diaspora-led ventures in sectors such as agriculture, manufacturing, and information technology have introduced innovative practices and technologies that enhance productivity and competitiveness. These businesses not only contribute to the local economy but also foster a culture of entrepreneurship that inspires others to pursue their own ventures.

From a sociological perspective, these entrepreneurial activities reflect the principles of social entrepreneurship, where business initiatives are driven by a commitment to social and economic development. By leveraging their skills, networks, and resources, diaspora entrepreneurs create value for their communities and contribute to the broader goal of nation-building.

2. *Impact on Rural Development and Infrastructure*

Diaspora-led entrepreneurial ventures have also had a significant impact on rural development and infrastructure in Punjab. Many diaspora members have invested in projects that improve access to basic services, such as clean water, electricity, and transportation, enhancing the quality of life for rural communities.

For instance, diaspora-funded initiatives have supported the construction of roads, bridges, and irrigation systems, enabling farmers to transport their goods to markets and access water for their crops. These infrastructure projects not only boost agricultural productivity but also create employment opportunities and stimulate local economic activity.

From a sociological perspective, these investments reflect the diaspora's commitment to participatory development, where local communities are actively involved in the planning and implementation of development projects. By empowering rural communities, the diaspora fosters a sense of ownership and agency, which is essential for sustainable development.

3. *Challenges and Opportunities for Diaspora Entrepreneurs*

Despite their contributions, diaspora entrepreneurs face several challenges in their efforts to drive economic development in Punjab. One major challenge is the lack of a supportive business environment, characterized by bureaucratic inefficiency, corruption, and inadequate infrastructure. These barriers can hinder the growth and sustainability of diaspora-led ventures, limiting their impact on the local economy.

Additionally, diaspora entrepreneurs may face cultural and social challenges, such as resistance from local communities or difficulties in navigating the complexities of doing business in Punjab. These challenges require a nuanced understanding of local contexts and a commitment to building trust and collaboration with local stakeholders.

From a sociological perspective, these challenges highlight the importance of social capital and network-building in overcoming barriers to entrepreneurship. By fostering relationships with local communities, policy-makers, and other stakeholders, diaspora entrepreneurs can create an enabling environment for their ventures and maximize their impact on development.

Impact on Nation-building

The role of remittances and diaspora-led entrepreneurial

ventures in Punjab's socio-economic development has significant implications for nation-building in contemporary contexts. By driving economic growth, creating jobs, and improving access to education and infrastructure, the diaspora contributes to the creation of a more inclusive and equitable society. Their efforts reflect the interconnectedness of global and local identities in a rapidly changing world, shaping the future of nation-building in the 21st century.

In today's globalized world, the role of younger generations in nation-building is deeply intertwined with their ability to leverage transnational networks and resources for socio-economic development. By investing in education, entrepreneurship, and infrastructure, they create a sense of unity and purpose that transcends national borders. These efforts not only address immediate challenges but also foster long-term resilience and sustainability, shaping the future of nation-building in the 21st century.

The role of remittances and diaspora-led entrepreneurial ventures in Punjab's socio-economic development highlights the transformative potential of transnational networks in shaping the future of nation-building. By addressing economic challenges, fostering innovation, and empowering communities, the diaspora contributes to the creation of a more inclusive and equitable society. Their efforts reflect the interconnectedness of global and local identities in a rapidly changing world, shaping the future of nation-building in the 21st century.

8.2 Transnational Networks and Collaboration

Transnational networks have become a cornerstone of the Punjabi diaspora's contributions to socio-economic development in Punjab. These networks, facilitated by diaspora organizations and collaborative initiatives, play a pivotal role in fostering economic ties, sharing knowledge, and driving development projects. From a sociological perspective, the role of transnational networks can be understood through frameworks such as social capital, global citizenship, and participatory development. This section explores the role of diaspora organizations in fostering economic ties and presents case studies of successful diaspora-driven projects, highlighting their implications for nation-building in contemporary contexts.

Transnational networks have now become crucial avenues through which the Punjabi diaspora maintains connectivity with their homelands, not just as family ties but also through economic cooperation, cultural retention, and political activism. These networks, established through family ties, communal associations, religious institutions (*gurdwaras* in particular), and professional societies, constitute the pillars of diasporic action in Punjab's development dynamics. They enable the exchange of ideas, skills, and capital that extend well beyond the conventional limits of remittances. The transnational connections, created by them, enable diaspora members to contribute to infrastructure schemes, schools, hospitals, and the modernization of agriculture in their hometowns and villages.

Diaspora associations, especially, have played a revolutionary role by institutionalizing philanthropy and creating forums for pooled development. For example, Punjabi communities in Canada, the UK, and the US have sponsored schools, vocational schools, and rural health projects, frequently reaching marginalized groups. Such collective interventions mark a change from individualized remittance-based charity to pooled, strategic investment in human and physical capital. Sociologically, this shift highlights the development of a type of global citizenship where diasporic agents take on the responsibility for socio-economic development of their home regions while promoting transparency, accountability, and participatory governance.

What is particularly effective about these networks is their capacity to cross-cultural and institutional divides. The diaspora members, who are themselves familiar with both the host countries' and the home country's operational standards, tend to emerge as intermediaries who can lead innovative technologies, contemporary management patterns, and universal development standards into local settings. Their engagement within educational curriculum adjustment, skill building programmes, as well as female empowerment activities are further reflection of their holistic pursuit of development. Thus, transnational cooperation not only strengthens local capacity but also reinforces values consonant with democratic engagement, social justice, and sustainability the very core principles of nation-building in a globalized world.

Role of Diaspora Organizations in Fostering Economic Ties

1. *Building Bridges between Punjab and the Global Economy*

Diaspora organizations serve as critical intermediaries that connect Punjab with the global economy. These organizations, often established and led by second and third-generation Punjabis, leverage their networks, expertise, and resources to promote trade, investment, and economic collaboration. By acting as bridges between Punjab and their host countries, they facilitate the flow of capital, technology, and knowledge, driving economic growth and development.

For example, organizations like the North American Punjabi Association (NAPA) and the Punjabi Chamber of Commerce have been instrumental in promoting business partnerships between Punjab and North America. These organizations organize trade delegations, business summits, and networking events that bring together entrepreneurs, policy-makers, and investors from both regions. Such initiatives not only boost economic activity but also create opportunities for knowledge exchange and innovation.

From a sociological perspective, these efforts reflect the principles of social capital, where networks and relationships are leveraged to achieve collective goals. By fostering economic ties, diaspora organizations strengthen the interconnectedness of global and local economies, contributing to the development of a more integrated and resilient global economy.

The organizations of the diaspora have also greatly widened Punjab's economic prospects by establishing extended channels of interface between international markets and domestic economies. The diaspora organizations commonly consist of extremely skilled professionals, entrepreneurs, and scholars who possess a sophisticated familiarity with both their host nations' economies and local Punjab needs. Their capacity for brokering between these two environments enables more focused and strategic investments in sectors like agribusiness, manufacturing, clean energy, and information technology. Diaspora organizations in this regard function not just as economic facilitators but as knowledge brokers, disseminating sophisticated skills and business practices to Punjab's entrepreneurial and industrial sectors.

In addition, such initiatives are not confined to big economic collaborations; numerous diaspora-led ventures aim to empower micro and small enterprises in rural and semi-urban Punjab. By providing mentorship, access to global markets, and financial support, diaspora organizations enable local entrepreneurs to overcome economic obstacles, thereby ensuring self-reliance and grassroots innovation. The participation of second and third-generation Punjabis in these efforts is especially noteworthy because it indicates a multigenerational commitment to the development of Punjab. Such younger diaspora members tend to have a cosmopolitan worldview and a sense of responsibility toward social justice and sustainable development.

In terms of nation-building, these engagements highlight the importance of the role played by civil society players in complementing state-driven development. When diaspora organizations join hands with local governance institutions, NGOs, and academic institutions, they facilitate the establishment of multi-stakeholder partnerships that deepen democratic engagement and ensure that development is responsive to community needs. These collaborative efforts bring about economic resilience, mitigate regional disparities, and advance a more participatory and equitable development paradigm, which are critical for the construction of a modern, inclusive, and globally integrated Indian nation.

2. *Promoting Entrepreneurship and Innovation*

Diaspora organizations also play a key role in promoting entrepreneurship and innovation in Punjab. Many of these organizations provide mentorship, funding, and technical support to aspiring entrepreneurs, enabling them to start and grow their businesses. By fostering a culture of entrepreneurship, they contribute to job creation, economic diversification, and sustainable development.

For instance, the Sikh Entrepreneurs Alliance (SEA) is a diaspora-led organization that supports Punjabi entrepreneurs through mentorship programmes, business incubators, and access to venture capital. These initiatives not only empower individuals to achieve economic self-sufficiency but also inspire others to pursue entrepreneurial ventures, creating a ripple effect that drives economic growth.

From a sociological perspective, this emphasis on entrepreneurship reflects the diaspora's commitment to participatory development, where individuals and communities are empowered to take ownership of their economic futures. By fostering innovation and creativity, diaspora organizations contribute to the development of a more dynamic and inclusive economy.

The encouragement of entrepreneurship and innovation on the part of diaspora organizations is a revolutionary strategy for Punjab's socio-economic growth. These organizations, based on transnational solidarity, give so much more than money they foster entrepreneurial attitudes by linking global knowledge with local desires. Diaspora-run incubators and innovation centres expose future Punjabi entrepreneurs to global best practices, digital technologies, and emerging market strategies, freeing them from the shackles of conventional occupation restrictions, particularly in agriculturally dependent areas. By promoting entrepreneurship in technology, renewable energy, education, and e-commerce, the diaspora is instrumental in realigning Punjab's economic direction in favour of sectors that have global economic competitiveness.

In addition, most diaspora-supported entrepreneurship initiatives are particularly aimed at women and disadvantaged groups, fostering social equality and inclusive development. This specific targeting erodes centuries-old exclusion from the formal economy and enables more representative economic leadership.

Embedding values of social entrepreneurship, which are business models working on solving local problems such as water shortage, waste disposal, or educational deficiencies, into these programmes ensures that profit-making is combined with social responsibility.

From a nation-building point of view, this empowerment through innovation redefines the diaspora's role from being passive benefactors to being active co-creators of development. It reflects a vision of decentralized and participatory development, where local entrepreneurs are envisioned as agents of change. In the long run, it generates a resilient economic culture in Punjab based on innovation, self-reliance, and interconnectedness with the world principles that align with India's overall ambitions for sustainable, inclusive, and equitable nation-building.

3. *Addressing Structural Barriers to Economic Development*

In addition to promoting economic ties and entrepreneurship, diaspora organizations also address structural barriers to economic development in Punjab. These barriers, which include bureaucratic inefficiency, corruption, and inadequate infrastructure, often hinder the growth and sustainability of businesses.

Diaspora organizations advocate for policy reforms and institutional changes that create a more enabling environment for economic activity. For example, the Punjab Governance Reforms Commission, which includes diaspora members, has played a crucial role in promoting transparency, accountability, and efficiency in governance. These efforts not only improve the business climate but also enhance the overall quality of life for local communities.

From a sociological perspective, this advocacy reflects the principles of global citizenship, where individuals take responsibility for the well-being of their communities and contribute to the collective good. By addressing structural barriers, diaspora organizations create a more equitable and just society, where economic opportunities are accessible to all.

Removal of structural impediments to economic progress is a necessary but usually underestimated contribution of the Punjabi diaspora to national development. Although financial investment and entrepreneurial support are important, unless systemic issues like bureaucratic red tape, uneven application of policy, and corruption is addressed, but sustained development continues to be held back. Diaspora groups, frequently wielding the credibility and influence acquired from their overseas presence, leverage their influence to drive institutional change and improved governance in Punjab. Their bicultural view grounded in local identity but tempered by international standards allows them to recognize inefficiencies and advocate pragmatic, actionable alternatives.

These groups often function as watchdogs and intermediaries, interfacing between the government and civil society so that development programmes reach the bottom. Through cooperation with universities, think tanks, and change-oriented bureaucrats, diaspora-initiated efforts are assisting in the process of making public services digital, reducing business license procedures, and making local governance more transparent. For example, efforts directed towards bringing about e-governance portals and mobile grievance redressal systems are the direct result of diaspora efforts. These initiatives not only enhance the ease of doing business but also empower common citizens by allowing them greater control over public systems.

From a sociological viewpoint, this involvement marks a shift towards a participatory model of development, in which governance is not left entirely in the hands of the state but becomes a collective responsibility. Diaspora individuals, as citizens of the world, are employing their resources, expertise, and networks to contribute to the dismantling of entrenched inequities and inefficiencies, bringing about a development model that is democratic, accountable, and inclusive. Such reforms, if they are sustained, prepare the foundations for sound institutions that can facilitate equitable economic growth, making the diaspora an integral partner in India's long-term nation-building process.

Case Studies of Successful Diaspora-driven Projects

1. *Punjab Water Forum: Addressing Water Scarcity*

The Punjab Water Forum, a diaspora-led initiative, has been at the forefront of addressing Punjab's water crisis, which is characterized by depleting groundwater levels and widespread pollution. The forum brings together experts, policy-makers, and local communities to promote sustainable water management practices, such as drip irrigation, crop diversification, and rainwater harvesting.

One of the forum's most successful projects is the promotion of direct seeding of rice (DSR), a water-efficient farming technique that reduces water consumption by up to 30 percent. Through awareness campaigns, training programmes, and financial incentives, the forum has encouraged thousands of farmers to adopt DSR, significantly reducing the strain on Punjab's water resources.

From a sociological perspective, this initiative exemplifies the power of transnational networks in addressing complex socio-economic challenges. By leveraging their expertise and resources, diaspora members facilitate the exchange of knowledge and best practices, enabling local communities to adopt innovative solutions to pressing problems.

2. *Punjab Rural Development Foundation: Empowering Rural Communities*

The Punjab Rural Development Foundation (PRDF), a diaspora-funded organization, has been instrumental in driving rural development in Punjab. The foundation focuses on improving access to education, healthcare, and livelihood opportunities for rural communities, particularly marginalized groups such as women and low-income families.

One of PRDF's flagship projects is the establishment of vocational training centres that provide skills training in areas such as tailoring, handicrafts, and computer literacy. These centres not only equip individuals with the skills needed to secure employment but also foster a sense of empowerment and self-reliance.

From a sociological perspective, this initiative reflects the principles of participatory development, where local communities are actively involved in the planning and implementation of development projects. By empowering rural communities, PRDF creates a sense of ownership and agency, which is essential for sustainable development.

3. *Punjab Health Initiative: Improving Access to Healthcare*

The Punjab Health Initiative (PHI), a diaspora-led project, has significantly improved access to healthcare for underserved populations in Punjab. The initiative includes mobile health units that travel to remote villages, offering diagnostic services, treatment, and health education. Additionally, PHI collaborates with local healthcare providers to build their capacity and improve the quality of care.

One of PHI's most impactful projects is the establishment of telemedicine centres that connect rural patients with specialists in urban areas. These centres not only improve access to specialized care but also reduce the burden on overcrowded urban hospitals.

From a sociological perspective, this initiative highlights the importance of social capital and network-building in addressing healthcare disparities. By leveraging their resources and expertise, diaspora members create a more inclusive and equitable healthcare system, where access to quality care is recognized as a fundamental human right.

Impact on Nation-building

The role of transnational networks and diaspora organizations in fostering economic ties and driving development projects has significant implications for nation-building in contemporary contexts. By promoting trade, investment, and entrepreneurship, these networks contribute to the creation of a more dynamic and inclusive economy. Their efforts reflect the interconnectedness of global and local identities in a rapidly changing world, shaping the future of nation-building in the 21st century.

In today's globalized world, the role of younger generations in nation-building is deeply intertwined with their ability to leverage transnational networks and resources for socio-economic development. By fostering economic ties, promoting innovation, and addressing structural barriers, they create a sense of unity and purpose that transcends national borders. These efforts not only address immediate challenges but also foster long-term resilience and sustainability, shaping the future of nation-building in the 21st century.

8.3 Challenges and Opportunities

The Punjabi diaspora's engagement in socio-economic development in Punjab is a powerful force for change, yet it is not without its complexities. While diaspora resources financial, intellectual, and social hold immense potential for driving progress, their effective utilization is often hindered by structural, cultural, and political barriers. From a sociological perspective, these challenges can be understood through frameworks such as transnationalism, power dynamics, and cultural hybridity. At the same time, these challenges also open doors for innovation, collaboration, and systemic transformation. This section delves into the barriers that impede the effective use of diaspora resources and explores the opportunities they create for reimagining development in Punjab.

Barriers to Effective Utilization of Diaspora Resources

1. *Structural Barriers: Bureaucratic Inefficiency and Corruption*

One of the most significant obstacles to leveraging diaspora resources is the structural inefficiency and corruption within Punjab's governance systems. Diaspora members often encounter bureaucratic hurdles when attempting to invest in or initiate development projects. Lengthy approval processes, lack of transparency, and demands for bribes can discourage even the most committed diaspora members from engaging in meaningful development work.

For instance, a diaspora-led initiative to establish a vocational training centre in Punjab may face delays due to bureaucratic red tape, or its impact may be diluted by corruption that diverts resources away from intended beneficiaries. These structural barriers not only frustrate diaspora efforts but also erode trust in local institutions, making it difficult to sustain long-term collaborations.

From a sociological perspective, these challenges reflect the broader issue of institutional weakness, where ineffective governance structures undermine the potential for collective action. Addressing these barriers requires systemic reforms that promote transparency, accountability, and efficiency in governance.

2. *Cultural Barriers: Misalignment of Values and Expectations*

Cultural differences between the diaspora and local communities can also hinder the effective utilization of resources. Diaspora members, particularly those born and raised abroad, may bring with them values, expectations, and approaches that do not align with local cultural norms and practices. This misalignment can lead to misunderstandings, resistance, and even conflict, undermining the success of development initiatives.

For example, a diaspora-led project promoting gender equality in rural Punjab may face resistance from local communities that adhere to traditional gender roles. Similarly, initiatives that emphasize individual entrepreneurship may clash with collectivist cultural values that prioritize community welfare over individual success.

From a sociological perspective, these cultural barriers highlight the complexities of cultural hybridity, where the negotiation of identity and values is an ongoing and contested process. To navigate these challenges, diaspora members must adopt a culturally sensitive approach that respects local traditions while advocating for progressive change.

3. *Political Barriers: Instrumentalization and Backlash*

The socio-political engagement of the diaspora is often subject to political instrumentalization, where their efforts are co-opted or manipulated by political actors for their own agendas. This instrumentalization can lead to a backlash against the diaspora, particularly when their interventions are perceived as interfering in local politics or undermining national sovereignty. For example, diaspora advocacy for human rights or environmental reforms may be framed as foreign interference by political elites seeking to maintain their power. This backlash can create a hostile environment for diaspora engagement, limiting their ability to effect meaningful change.

From a sociological perspective, this challenge reflects the contested nature of transnationalism, where the boundaries between local and global actors are constantly negotiated. To navigate this complexity, the diaspora must adopt a collaborative and non-partisan approach that prioritizes the interests of local communities over political agendas.

4. *Economic Barriers: Dependency and Uneven Distribution*

While remittances and diaspora investments have a positive impact on Punjab's economy, they also have limitations that need to be addressed. One major challenge is the dependency on diaspora resources, which can create a culture of complacency and discourage local entrepreneurship. In some cases, families may rely solely on remittances for their livelihood, rather than seeking opportunities for economic self-sufficiency.

Additionally, the uneven distribution of diaspora resources can exacerbate existing inequalities, as wealthier households are more likely to receive larger amounts of money. This can create disparities in access to education, healthcare, and other resources, further marginalizing vulnerable groups.

From a sociological perspective, these challenges highlight the need for a more balanced approach to development, where diaspora resources are complemented by policies that promote local entrepreneurship, job creation, and social equity.

Opportunities for Reimagining Development

1. *Leveraging Technology for Inclusive Development*

One of the most promising opportunities for overcoming barriers to diaspora engagement is the use of technology. Digital platforms, such as social media, crowdfunding websites, and telemedicine services, can facilitate the flow of resources, knowledge, and expertise between the diaspora and local communities.

For example, diaspora members can use crowdfunding platforms to raise funds for development projects, bypassing traditional bureaucratic channels. Similarly, telemedicine services can connect rural patients with diaspora healthcare professionals, improving access to quality care.

From a sociological perspective, the use of technology reflects the principles of digital transnationalism, where digital networks enable the diaspora to maintain a connection to their ancestral homeland while also engaging with global audiences. By leveraging technology, the diaspora can create more inclusive and participatory development initiatives that empower local communities.

2. *Building Collaborative Networks for Systemic Change*

Another opportunity lies in building collaborative networks that bring together diaspora members, local communities, and policy-makers to address systemic barriers to development. These networks can facilitate the exchange of ideas, resources, and best practices, enabling stakeholders to work together towards common goals.

For instance, a collaborative network focused on education could bring together diaspora educators, local teachers, and policy-makers to design and implement innovative educational programmes. By fostering collaboration, these networks can create a more enabling environment for development, where the expertise and resources of the diaspora are effectively utilized.

From a sociological perspective, these collaborative networks reflect the principles of participatory development, where diverse stakeholders are actively involved in the planning and implementation of development initiatives. By fostering collaboration, the diaspora can create a more inclusive and equitable society, where the benefits of development are shared by all.

3. *Promoting Social Entrepreneurship for Sustainable Development*

Social entrepreneurship, which combines business principles with a commitment to social and environmental impact, presents another opportunity for reimagining development in Punjab. Diaspora members can leverage their skills, networks, and resources to establish social enterprises that address pressing socio-economic challenges, such as poverty, unemployment, and environmental degradation.

For example, a diaspora-led social enterprise could focus on promoting sustainable agriculture by providing farmers with training, resources, and market linkages. By addressing both economic and environmental challenges, these enterprises can create a more sustainable and resilient economy.

From a sociological perspective, social entrepreneurship reflects the principles of social innovation, where new ideas and approaches are used to address complex social problems. By promoting social entrepreneurship, the diaspora can create a more dynamic and inclusive economy, where the benefits of development are shared by all.

Impact on Nation-building

The challenges and opportunities associated with the utilization of diaspora resources have significant implications for nation-building in contemporary contexts. While structural, cultural, and political barriers hinder the effective utilization of diaspora resources, they also present opportunities for innovation, collaboration, and systemic change. By leveraging technology, building collaborative networks, and promoting social entrepreneurship, the diaspora can overcome these barriers and contribute to the creation of a more inclusive and equitable society.

In today's globalized world, the role of younger generations in nation-building is deeply intertwined with their ability to navigate the complexities of transnationalism and cultural hybridity. By addressing these challenges and seizing these opportunities, they can create a sense of unity and purpose that transcends national borders. These efforts not only address immediate challenges but also foster long-term resilience and sustainability, shaping the future of nation-building in the 21st century.

8.4 Challenges and Opportunities

The Punjabi diaspora ranks among the most important transnational communities that have made substantial contributions in both their host and homeland nations. Their participation in economic, social, and cultural activities has produced ground-breaking effects in various areas like education, healthcare, business, and political activism. In spite of all their innovative work in nation-building, many socio-cultural, economic, and political obstacles hinder the proper utilization of their resources. These barriers are deeply rooted within structural institutions, generational changes, political struggles, and cultural negotiations. A sociological analysis of these challenges reveals how historical and contemporary factors structure the Punjabi diaspora's connection with their homeland.

Structural and Institutional Barriers

One of the core challenges facing diaspora involvement is the lack of institutional mechanisms that facilitate their contributions. As important as remittances and philanthropy are to the Punjab economy, bureaucratic barriers, poor policy clarity, and irregular government outreach tend to discourage long-term involvement. Much of the second and third-generation diaspora population faces difficulties with property ownership, business regulation, and political representation.

From a sociological perspective, Pierre Bourdieu's social capital theory describes how networks, trust, and access to institutions influence economic and social exchange (Bourdieu, 1986). Punjabi diaspora is often severed from the formal state institutions in India, resulting in inefficiencies and corruption in economic and charitable activities. In spite of schemes such as the Overseas Citizenship of India (OCI) scheme, legal barriers in terms of landownership, taxation, and voting rights still constrain the maximum potential of diaspora involvement (Sharma, 2015). In addition, though the Punjabi Non-Resident Indian (NRI) Commission was instituted to cater to diaspora issues, it is still mired in bureaucratic inefficiencies. Failure to institutionalize diaspora investments in long-term development projects translates into episodic and un-systematic contributions instead of strategic, long-term involvement.

Generational Shifts and Cultural Identity

The changing dynamics of the Punjabi diaspora's relationship with the homeland are also influenced by the generational difference. The migrants of the first generation had a strong emotional and economic connection to Punjab, while the second and third generations are usually plagued by identity and cultural assimilation problems. The disconnect between generations determines their readiness to engage in development initiatives beyond nostalgia trips and cultural tourism.

Erik Erikson's theory of identity formation is a helpful prism for understanding such a transition, highlighting the twin struggles of identity as faced by diaspora youth who grow up in transnational locations (Erikson, 1968). While previous generations focused on economic remittances and investment in infrastructure projects, younger diaspora individuals are more involved in digital activism, global human rights movements, and transnational campaigning as opposed to direct investments in Punjab (Singh & Kaur, 2020). The growing dependence on social media activism enables virtual involvement in homeland issues, but its physical contribution to economic development is limited.

Political and Socio-economic Barriers

Diaspora relations tend to get caught up in political rhetoric about nationalism, regionalism, and past injustices. The Punjabi diaspora, most notably in Canada, the UK, and the US, have contributed to narratives of Sikh identity and self-governance, which have been contentious with the Indian state. Political distrust, along with state monitoring and controlling policies, has resulted in tensions that interfere with smooth cooperation.

Sociologically, Benedict Anderson's imagined communities shed light on the way diaspora communities imagine their homelands, idealizing historical and cultural connections that are not necessarily representative of the current situation (Anderson, 1983). The Khalistan movement has also added to the complexities of diaspora-state relations, with resulting disjointed engagement strategies favouring ideological identification over cohesive developmental agendas (Tatla, 1999).

Economically, while being among the richest migrant groups, members of the Punjabi diaspora experience investment constraints arising from land conflicts, bureaucratic uncertainty, and lax legal enforcement of property rights. Punjab's economy, which remains predominantly agrarian, has found it difficult to absorb high-tech manufacturing and innovation-based businesses started by diaspora businesspeople. The absence of institutional mechanisms for facilitating knowledge and technology transfers is an additional limiting factor for the scope of sustainable development.

Shifts in Diaspora Engagement: A New Nation-Building Approach

The new generation of the Punjabi diaspora views nation-building differently compared to the previous generation. Rather than only concentrating on remittances and big-ticket investments, their involvement is marked by social entrepreneurship, skill-based volunteering, and advocacy for policy changes.

Social Entrepreneurship: Young diaspora individuals are establishing ventures focused on farmer suicides, environmental degradation, and gender imbalance in Punjab. In contrast to conventional donation-oriented models, they focus on sustainable solutions that drive local self-sufficiency and autonomy (Gill, 2021).

Skill-based Volunteering: Medical doctors, teachers, and technical experts from the diaspora are increasingly being engaged in mentorship schemes and skill-transfer exercises. Initiatives such as the Punjab Youth Leaders Program (PYLP) are organized platforms for building capacity over direct financial aid. Policy Advocacy and Digital Mobilization: The 2020-2021 farmers' protests showed the potential of digital activism among the Punjabi diaspora. Through political lobbying, media campaigns, and crowdfunding, diaspora youth played a pivotal role in framing international discourses on Punjab's agrarian crisis (Kumar, 2022). While this engagement does not necessarily translate into economic investment, it has intensified global debate about Punjab's socio-economic issues.

Gender and Diaspora Contributions

Diaspora participation has traditionally been male-dominated, with initial migration flows being predominantly Punjabi men who migrated for work. But growing female migration has transformed diaspora contributions, especially in education, healthcare, and grassroots activism. Diaspora women are more actively engaged in social welfare initiatives, feminist movements, and transnational advocacy (Kaur, 2020). Intersectionality theory (Crenshaw, 1989) from a feminist sociological point of view emphasizes the way in which Punjabi women in the diaspora negotiate layers of identity and participation. Gender biases in host and home nations persist to circumscribe their visibility and influence in economic choice and political activism.

9

Findings and Conclusion

Findings from the Interview Schedule

The information gathered in interviews with the respondents from Bathinda, Barnala, and Jalandhar, currently settled in Canada, the US, Australia, the UK, and Italy, brings to the fore a rich and multidimensional understanding of the demographic, cultural, economic, and political patterns of the Punjabi diaspora. Both continuities as well as change within the diasporic phenomenon, specifically delineated by generations, occupational variance, and transnationality, are revealed through the findings.

The diaspora in question is overwhelmingly young, with a large proportion of those in early adulthood. This demographic pattern indicates that migration remains a preferred pathway for young Punjabis looking for education, work, or general life prospects overseas. Older generations are also present, reflecting both new waves of migration and permanent settlement. The gender makeup reflects a relatively balanced presence, with women playing an increasingly active role in migration and diaspora existence, thus challenging conventional gender roles and indicating changing socio-cultural norms among Punjabi families.

Geographically, the diaspora is dispersed across leading English-speaking nations, with Canada proving to be a highly desirable destination given its established Punjabi communities and welcoming immigration policies. The presence of Punjabis in Italy highlights the increasing attractiveness of non-English-speaking European countries, in which economic prospects in agriculture and small industries have attracted migrants. The presence of first, second, and third-generation migrants shows the established nature of the diaspora, in which each generation negotiates identity, belonging, and cultural preservation in different ways.

Occupationally, the diaspora is diverse. Members are working in both white-collar occupations like IT, healthcare, and administration, and blue-collar jobs in construction, transportation, and manufacturing. Students also indicate education as a force driving migration. This diversity indicates both upward mobility and the continuation of traditional labour migration streams. The data shows differences in cultural attachment. Whereas for some there is strong or medium attachment to Punjabi culture along the lines of language, norms, and religious festivals, minimal attachment is manifest among others, especially the youth or subsequent generations. This depicts the effect of host society assimilation, though also the endeavours by community organizations as well as online forums, for the maintenance of cultural identity across borders.

Participation in culture is variable, some are actively involved in Punjabi festivals and art forms and some are at arm's length from them. The use of Punjabi in preserving identity is understood by many, but others are indifferent or negative in response due to pragmatic issues surrounding integration and applicability. There is also seen to be a change in response among younger generations towards traditions, and responses range from great cultural pride to sentiments of disconnection and disappearing traditions.

Economically, the diaspora has strong links with Punjab in the form of remittances, investment, and support networks. These economic and social links are viewed as critical to the development of Punjab. Government use of remittances is viewed with varying degrees of efficacy and effectiveness, as well as doubts on whether diaspora-initiated initiatives have concrete effects. Diaspora voting rights are viewed with differing opinions, with emotional ties being at odds with legal-political possibilities. However, the diaspora is regarded as having an impact on Punjab's political agenda and development agenda through advocacy, investment, and transnational activism.

Lastly, although many affirm deep emotional connections with Punjab and a desire to return should things get better, some are firmly settled elsewhere. These observations point to the contradictory nature of diaspora identity rooted and yet mobile, nostalgic and adaptable by generational, cultural, economic, and geopolitical influences.

Findings from the Secondary Data Analysis

The investigation of Ajmer Rode's literary history, Anita Lerche's music career, and the online space of Punjabi identity formation yields a dynamic and changing transnational cultural field. These case studies, informed by media analysis and digital ethnography, illustrate that diasporic identity is not a fixed heritage but a dynamically reconstituted phenomenon positioned at the junctures of art, memory, migration, and media technologies. This shifting identity is sustained and reconfigured by varied cultural practices that stretch across physical and virtual geographies.

One of the key sociological discoveries is the pivotal role played by cultural production in sustaining identity among diasporic populations. Ajmer Rode's work as a playwright and writer is representative of diasporic intellectual interest in homeland histories and shared memory. His writing not only captures the plight of dislocation and cultural displacement but also acts as a vehicle for challenging exclusionary policies and institutional racism traditionally faced by the Punjabi diaspora in Canada. Likewise, Anita Lerche's engagement with Punjabi folk traditions, though from non-diasporic origins, illustrates how transcultural engagement can globalize and reconfigure Punjabi identity outside ethnic confines. This undermines essentialist conceptions of cultural authenticity, demonstrating instead that cultural identity is performative and negotiated within local and global contexts.

The analysis of digital media also underscores the centrality of online spaces in maintaining and reconfiguring diasporic identity. Social media has become a performative and participatory space where diasporic people particularly youth create hybrid identities that combine their ethnic origins with the cultural idioms of host societies. The increased popularity of Punjabi fusion music, diasporic film, and multilingual online content implies a media landscape that accommodates fluid, syncretic identities. This is reflective of what academics refer to as "glocalization", a process in which global cultural flows are brought back home through community-specific practices. YouTube, Instagram, and Facebook are not entertainment sites alone; they are cultural spaces in which issues of identity, belonging, and political awareness are actively negotiated.

Another important discovery is the development of digital memory as a collective consciousness tool. Digital archives, like the Punjab Digital Library and diaspora-initiated media websites, provide a virtual storehouse of community memory and act as counter-narratives to dominant historiographies. These sites record both past experiences such as the Komagata Maru incident and current political movements, such as international support for the Indian farmers' protests. By doing so, they affirm a transnational moral economy, through which diaspora groups engage the political and cultural affairs of the homeland while impacting socio-political discourse in host nations. Such two-way engagement aligns with the contention that diaspora communities are not mere subjects of cultural loss but rather are agents of cultural and political continuity.

Furthermore, digital ethnography demonstrates how diasporic media spaces serve as activist platforms where advocacy on issues of migration, racial justice, and Sikh identity politics can take place. Through these online platforms, mobilization by the community that crosses borders becomes possible, allowing diaspora actors to shape policy, raise awareness, and build solidarity. Such insights highlight the transformative capacity of digital media in cultural preservation, political activism, and identity negotiation.

Findings from the Primary Data Analysis

The case stories highlighted here, based on primary field interviews with young people from Northeast India, especially those belonging to the tribal population, provide important observations about the socio-cultural changes brought about by digital globalization, emigration, and algorithmic social media involvement. The case studies mirror a shifting cultural landscape of identity, in which classic affiliations are being reshaped by East Asian, Western, and pan-Indian mass media cultures. The results depict the complex interaction between media consumption habits, language use, identity construction, and intergenerational dynamics.

First, a major sociological discovery is the advent of digital proximity as a revolutionary force that determines cultural affinities. The exposure of the respondents to Korean, Chinese, and Western digital content primarily through platforms like TikTok, Instagram, YouTube, and Reddit has generated affective communities that cross geographical boundaries. Through frequent participation in online fan cultures and peer networks, young people express a notion of belonging that is increasingly global, culturally oriented instead of their indigenous heritage. It is such a de-territorialized cultural identity in which affective connections and media-driven aspirations become the core factor in creating belonging.

Secondly, the linguistic transformation noticed among respondents is a key indicator of this cultural shift. English, which is already pervasive in institutional and professional environments, is yet more supported by the digital media, while Korean linguistic features such as popular K-pop phrases or the use of Hangul are being incorporated into virtual communication. Therefore, the proficiency and use of tribal languages have significantly diminished. This observation aligns with concerns in sociolinguistics over language attrition, especially among marginalized linguistic groups in contact with powerful global languages. Lack of tribal language content on both mainstream and online media exacerbates this process as young people discover few opportunities or incentives to retain or use their native languages.

Third, the respondents reflect a perceived cultural deficit resulting from the underrepresentation of their communities in new media. The lack of dynamic, contemporary representations of indigenous existence in film, fashion, music, and social media leaves a void that is increasingly being filled by foreign cultural narratives. This highlights the representational imbalance experienced by tribal communities, which leads to cultural alienation and the idealization of foreign cultures, seen as modern or desirable. Young people are not just passive consumers but active producers reworking their identity performances in the virtual world, usually at the expense of traditional cultural participation.

Moreover, the study finds that intergenerational cultural dissonance is expanding. While parents and older generations advocate cultural preservation and heritage-based practices, younger generations tend to view these practices as incompatible with their digital lives and peer pressures. The compromise between modernity and tradition takes the form of cultural hybridity, in which aspects of tribal identity are held in reserve internally but infrequently expressed outwardly in ordinary social interaction, particularly in urban or virtual environments. Such hybridity can easily turn superficial, though, if not accompanied by intentional efforts of cultural revitalization.

Lastly, the results highlight the contribution of social media algorithms to cultural exposure. The repeated viewing of East Asian and Western content by the respondents is not just a function of preference but also algorithmic reinforcement, which systematically demotes local content. This process requires more academic and policy focus on platform regulation, content diversity, and the necessity of strategic digital interventions that can facilitate indigenous representation online.

The analysis of primary data presents significant insight into the mechanisms through which social media and digital globalization are recasting cultural identities, notably amongst the Punjabi diaspora. Such an analysis is invaluable for grasping the intersections through which transnational communities have intersecting points that include global digital content, media consumption controlled by algorithms, and the fluidizing dynamics of cultural belonging. The research identifies how these processes are impacting the Punjabi diaspora's identity formation, sociality, and contributions to nation-building, particularly against the backdrop of a more globalized world.

One of the major revelations from the analysis is the influential power of digital proximity in forming cultural affinities. Punjabi diaspora youth, especially in the West, have been exposed to global cultural goods through social media sites such as TikTok, Instagram, and YouTube, which offer access to varied cultural narratives from East Asia, the West, and other parts of the world. Availability of such content with ease has led to the creation of affective communities that dissolve national and geographical borders. This phenomenon of virtual proximity has established a transnational space in which identity construction is being shaped more by global media use than by customary, locally-located culture. The outcome is a malleable cultural identity constructed more through media-influenced aspirations and peer networks than by embedded, heritage-based affiliations.

For the Punjabi diaspora, this trend is especially acute. Whilst staying connected with their heritage, much of the young membership in the community is proclaiming a cultural hybridity in which there co-exists with their Punjabi identity an uptake of world-wide trends. Such fluidity in identity is augmented further through participation in international fan cultures like that of Bollywood and K-pop as well as Western entertainment. This fusion of global and local is indicative of a larger cultural hybridization process, whereby diaspora communities reconcile multiple cultural influences, blending them into everyday life and self-expression.

In addition, the results show a marked shift in the use of language. English, already a powerful language in working and educational contexts, is further solidified by digital media platforms, which exist primarily in English. Moreover, younger generations of the Punjabi diaspora are also incorporating new linguistic markers, like popular K-pop phrases or American colloquialisms, into their online communication. This shift in language is indicative of larger trends of language assimilation, wherein local languages like Punjabi are being increasingly pushed aside by global languages like English. This erosion of language is an immediate result of the global media context focusing on the globalized languages and cultural histories, further diminishing the use of Punjabi in mundane interactions. The declining linguistic ability of the younger generation is a problem for the continuity of cultural practices and the handing down of heritage in the diaspora.

In addition, the absence of indigenous representations within international digital media aggravates a feeling of cultural lack among the Punjabi diaspora. As seen in other marginalized peoples, the failure of mainstream media to present positive, up-to-date images of Punjabi life in music, film, or fashion leaves a vacuum that is typically filled by foreign cultural ideals. This results in a process of cultural alienation in which younger diaspora members are more likely to romanticize and identify with global, frequently Western or East Asian, cultures that are represented as modern and aspirational. Although the Punjabi diaspora still observes their cultural festivals and traditions, these may become increasingly disconnected from their daily digital lives, where global cultures fill the social media space.

Concurrently, the research also identifies the generation gap that is increasingly evident among the diaspora. Older generations, being generally more attached to conventional modes of cultural expression, believe in the preservation of culture through heritage practices, language, and religious practices. Younger generations, exposed to the global media environment, perceive these conventional practices as antiquated or incompatible with their digital existence and peer relationships. This cross-generational cultural dissonance is particularly problematic for diaspora populations because it challenges cultural heritage transmission. Yet, in doing so, it offers a chance for revitalization of culture through the formation of hybrid modes of identity combining modern and traditional elements in a more compartmentalized or selective manner.

These changes are compounded by the influence of social media algorithms. The algorithmic specificity of online content delivery, where algorithms promote content based on past interactions, systematically exposes audiences to global and mainstream media and marginalizes local and indigenous content. For the Punjabi diaspora, this translates to local cultural narratives often being pushed to the margins of online spaces, depriving the younger generation of opportunities to engage with their heritage online. This raises an urgent question for the future of Punjabi cultural representation in the global digital space. Therefore, policy interventions are required that govern the digital media space to promote a more pluralistic representation of cultures, including the Punjabi diaspora, so that young people have access to both global and locally appropriate content.

Conclusion

The sociological analysis of the Punjabi diaspora from Bathinda, Barnala, and Jalandhar settled in Canada, the US, Australia, the UK, and Italy provides in-depth perspectives on the migration, settlement, identity negotiation, and transnational processes. Based on both primary data collected using interview schedules as well as secondary sources, the study brings to light the dynamic character of Punjabi diasporic communities towards demographic diversity, occupational diversification, cultural negotiation, and political ambivalence. From an analytical perspective, one can see that the diaspora is not one homogenous block but a fluid and multilevel social entity with varying ambitions, levels of identification with the cultural heritage, and levels of identification with the homeland.

Perhaps one of the most important results of this study is the generational layering of the diaspora, and how this is critical to understand cultural retention as well as the construction of identity. First-generation migrants tend to have a greater attachment to Punjabi cultural practices, language, and traditions because of their real-life experiences in Punjab. Second- and third-generation members, however, show disparate levels of affiliation anything from active cultural participation to partial or near-total assimilation into host societies. This generational difference is a natural and sociologically important one, indicating the fluidity of diasporic identity, which is conditioned by exposure to other socio-cultural and educational systems, language environments, and peer cultures in host countries.

The occupational profile also highlights the changing class locations of the diaspora. Several have shifted into professional occupations like information technology, health services, and education, reflecting a level of mobility. Others are occupied in blue-collar work, confirming the continuation of older migratory patterns based on economic need. Such distinctions not only shape the economic position of members of the diaspora but also determine their ability to invest in cultural reproduction. White-collar professionals, for example, might have better access to cultural institutions, communal activities, and web channels that assist in preserving links to Punjabi heritage. On the other hand, members of the manual labour occupations may not enjoy as many such opportunities because of prolonged working hours, economic limitations, or spatial segregation in their receiving societies.

Culturally, the diaspora has several modes of engagement with Punjabi identity. While some actively involve themselves in festivals, traditional music, dance, and food practices, others have only a symbolic or nostalgia-related engagement. The decline of cultural customs among certain members, particularly the young, is reflective of the larger issue of cultural sustainability in the time of globalization and cultural homogenization. Language becomes a particularly important marker of identity but also a point of concern. While most of the respondents identify Punjabi as essential to cultural continuity, others are hesitant and ambivalent because of practical impediments like the lack of institutional facilitation, the absence of Punjabi in formal education in foreign countries, and a sense of irrelevance in their daily lives.

The results also attest to the political and economic power of the diaspora. Even though they have restricted voting and political representation in Punjab, diaspora members are important discursively in terms of remittances, investments, philanthropy, and advocacy. Their discursive power is now more evident in the socio-economic environment of Punjab, as many give back to healthcare, education, business growth, and infrastructure. There is, however, a discernible gap in trust and openness between diaspora communities and state institutions, specifically concerning the utilization of remitted funds and the performance of diaspora-led programmes. This necessitates increased accountability and participatory frameworks to encourage mutual trust.

One of the repeated themes within the data is the duality of identity, where diaspora members tend to negotiate between their homelands of origin and their adopted countries. Some of the participants feel an intimate emotional and cultural affiliation with Punjab, while others feel more identified with their host countries or have an equilibrated dual identification. This duality is key to the subjectivity of diaspora in the contemporary world. It also expresses the multifaceted process of identification that is neither totally anchored in tradition nor completely inserted into modernity.

With regard to reintegration, a significant percentage of respondents indicate a desire to go back to Punjab under better socio-economic conditions. This indicates the ongoing emotional attraction of the homeland and holds promise for reverse migration if there are infrastructural, political, and economic reforms. However, for others, the choice to remain abroad is influenced by stability, opportunities, and family relationships in host nations. Therefore, return migration continues to be a conditional desire, not an inevitable reality.

With these results, some steps need to be taken in order to secure greater inclusion of the Punjabi diaspora in cultural development and preservation activities. Institutionalized means of engaging with the diaspora need to be established through specific government agencies or diaspora councils. These avenues can be used for dialogue, coordination, and the directing of resources toward development and cultural activities in Punjab.

Secondly, education in the Punjabi language has to be consolidated both within India and abroad. Community schools, online studies, and cultural internships in destination countries can facilitate the retention of linguistic heritage among the youth. Punjabi universities and diaspora organizations can also be encouraged to collaborate in language learning and academic exchange.

Third, cultural diplomacy needs to be pursued. Cultural centres, *gurudwaras*, and diaspora organizations overseas need to be nourished and remain centres of cultural activity. These institutions can be used to promote music festivals, dance classes, storytelling sessions, and classes in traditional arts to preserve cultural practices. Media, particularly digital media such as YouTube, podcasts, and social media, can be effective means of intergenerational transmission of culture and for building a collective diasporic awareness.

Fourth, economic linkages need to be made transparent and inclusive. Diaspora investment in property, education, and health needs to be acknowledged, but more significantly, it is necessary to evolve mechanisms so that such investments result in equitable and sustainable progress. Public-private partnerships between diaspora businesspeople and the Punjab state machinery can be commenced with well-identified goals and monitoring mechanisms.

Fifth, inclusive political participation and representation have to be nurtured. Even though legal constraints bar voting for most overseas citizens, other modes of consultation, including diaspora advisory boards, constituency-based representation, or internet-based participatory platforms, may be considered for incorporating diaspora voices into policy-making. Such measures can overcome alienation and strengthen the concept of collective responsibility for Punjab's future.

Finally, the diaspora's sociopolitical potential needs to be activated through transnational activism and coalition-building. Activism across issues such as farmer welfare, green growth, gender equity, and human rights in Punjab tends to resonate widely with diaspora members. Solidarity networks based on geography can be used to reinforce these causes and foster a more active, responsible, and morally responsible mode of diasporic citizenship.

In conclusion, the Bathinda, Barnala, and Jalandhar Punjabi diaspora though heterogeneous in composition and experience is an integral part of Punjab's socio-cultural and economic existence. It is both a cultural ambassador and as economic contributor, mediating between local and global spaces. For such a connection to flourish meaningfully, there must be a conscious and comprehensive system of engagement established, one that not only acknowledges the diaspora as benefactors or nostalgic witnesses, but also as co-creators of a dynamic and emergent Punjabi identity in the 21st century. Sociologically speaking, this means addressing the diaspora as an active social force, one which is capable of shaping, saving, and changing the cultural narrative of Punjab across borders and generations.

The initial Punjabi migration, especially that of the colonial and post-colonial eras, cannot be seen as simply the physical movement of people. It has to be placed within a wider sociological context that explains historical inequalities, colonial economic imperatives, caste and class relations, and the great geopolitical break of the Partition of India in 1947. These patterns of migration, determined first through the commands of British imperial states and subsequently through post-independence national trends, were rooted deeply within trajectories of dispossession, state-making, and remaking of collective forms. Knowledge of the early migratory streams of Punjabis makes possible a more balanced view of the modern dynamics of the diaspora and its intricate socio-economic and cultural dynamics.

Among the strongest influences on Punjabi migration in the early times was the British colonial policy of enlisting particular ethnic groups into the military. Colonial categorization of Sikhs, and especially Punjabis, as a "martial race" helped build a loyal, supposedly disciplined category of subjects good for imperial army deployment. Racially and culturally essentialist in character, this conception had no foundation in anthropological fact but was, instead, a political and administrative device used to act in imperial favour. Rural Punjab, which was already marked by agrarian hierarchies and restricted economic prospects, became a principal recruitment pool for the British Indian Army. Punjabi men found military service to be relatively secure sources of income and bestowed prestige in their communities. The soldiers were frequently sent to imperial peripheries stretching from Burma and the Middle East to East Africa and Europe, especially during the World Wars. This deployment helped generate the mobility of people, remittances, and ideas between Punjab and the global world, establishing early roots of diaspora networks that eventually supported diaspora populations. The sociological effects of military recruitment were double-edged. On the one hand, it exposed Punjabis from rural areas to new ways of thinking and altered local economies through remittances. Conversely, it reestablished a reliance on colonial patronage and positioned Punjabis in systems of imperial domination.

In addition to military recruitment, the administration also made large-scale labour migration out of Punjab possible. Punjabis, specifically those from landless or lower-caste groups, were organized as indentured or contract labourers for infrastructure development such as railways, canals, and plantations. It frequently led them to other regions in India as well as colonies in Southeast Asia, Africa, and the Caribbean. These movements of labour were normally coercive, exploitative, and offered no social mobility. In contrast to military migration, where relative status and resources were available, labour migration exposed people to inhuman working conditions and institutional marginalization. The colonial economy prospered on such racial labour that brought whole communities down to the status of instruments of economic exploitation. Such proletarianization of rural Punjabi labour undermined traditional forms of social organization and facilitated the shift from agrarian self-reliance towards wage dependence. It also created new diasporic cultures based on common conditions of exploitation and collective action. These initial labour migrations, though sometimes neglected, were a prime factor in the construction of diasporic consciousness and solidarity.

The trauma and displacement caused by the Partition of India in 1947 represented a turning point in Punjabi migration history. With the partition of the Punjab region between India and Pakistan, there were record levels of communal violence, mass killings, and forced displacement. Over 14 million people were displaced, and up to 2 million lost their lives in the violence that followed the drawing of the Radcliffe Line. For Punjabis, who were at the epicenter of this humanitarian catastrophe, the rupture was not only territorial but deeply personal and communal. Long-standing bonds of coexistence between Hindus, Muslims, and Sikhs were abruptly and violently severed. Whole villages were vacated, women were abducted and violated, and families were dispersed over newly created borders. The sociological impact of the Partition migration was gigantic and profound. It created permanent scars in the collective consciousness of Punjabis and forged diasporic accounts based on trauma, loss, and nostalgia.

For most, the experience of Partition still shapes the way identity is negotiated in India and elsewhere. Partition stories reconstructed through oral histories, literature, and family recollections have come to form a core part of diasporic identity, particularly in individuals who left soon after 1947. They not only maintain memory of the past but also influence the way that later generations comprehend their heritage and sense of belonging. Nevertheless, the material effects of Partition were not evenly allocated. While some upper-caste landowning groups were awarded compensatory land and state assistance in India, *Dalits* and lower-caste refugees, who were marginalized groups, were frequently relegated to refugee camps or slums. They were often pushed into low-wage, insecure jobs in cities such as Delhi, Amritsar, and Ludhiana. These groups experienced triple jeopardy: loss of homeland, economic marginalization, and social exclusion in the newly created nation-state. The unevenness of post-Partition rehabilitation helped to stratify migrant experiences and determine subsequent migration paths.

During the post-Partition era, Punjabi migration persisted, now spurred by long-term structural issues instead of immediate violence. The post-Partition agrarian economy of East Punjab, even with the benefit of the Green Revolution of the 1960s and 70s, remained highly unequal. The mechanization of agriculture, although raising productivity, also decreased the need for labour and widened land inequality. Small and marginal farmers, particularly belonging to lower castes, were increasingly being driven to the margins of economic survival. This generated powerful push factors for international migration. Punjab's people, especially from districts such as Jalandhar, Hoshiarpur, and Ludhiana, started emigrating to the United Kingdom, Canada, and the United States through labour, student, and family reunion programmes. The migrations were stratified on the basis of caste, class, and gender. Upper-caste Jat Sikhs with landholdings, education, and money could more easily maneuver immigration structures, while *Dalit* and landless households were confronted with barriers that appeared impossible to overcome.

The sociological consequences of this stratified migration are profound. Diasporic Punjabi populations are not uniform; they are differentiated internally by historical privilege, access to capital, and cultural capital. While some in the diaspora formed prosperous businesses, attained political representation, and gained symbolic status as "model minorities", others languished in low-wage labour markets, experienced racial discrimination, and battled social mobility. Migration then became a double-edged phenomenon, offering mobility and dignity to some, while reinforcing patterns of precarity for others. Successive waves of migrants, over time, built upon the foundations created by early migrants to construct large transnational networks that fuelled subsequent flows of migration. Remittances remade rural Punjab, enabling families to invest in landholdings, education, and social rituals. But this process tended to be exclusionary. Success by migrants turned into a new type of social status, creating what some academics refer to as a "migration culture" in which migrating itself was celebrated, independent of success or failure. This reinforced migration hopes for young people even if chances at home were available.

Finally, then, the pioneering migration of Punjabis in the colonial and post-colonial eras needs to be conceived as a historically embedded process conditioned by imperialisms, structural inequalities, social hierarchies, and mass displacement. Migration was never ever an untrammeled voluntaristic act but was thoroughly conditioned by regimes of domination, survival struggles, and the quest for dignity. These pioneering migration streams left permanent effects economic, cultural, and political on sending and receiving areas. They gave rise to the development of complex diasporic identities that are based on trauma, resilience, and transnational belonging. The Punjabi diaspora in the present owes a great deal to these early migrations, yet it also remains embroiled in their legacies, notably concerning internal inequalities and competing narratives of identity. Stratification of migratory experiences on the basis of caste, class, gender, and religion is an ongoing aspect of the diaspora. Hence, a sociologically critical response should not just rejoice in diasporic success but also critically examine the exclusions and silences that surround them.

On the basis of these observations, policy interventions addressing both the legacy of the past and the realities of the present are necessary for migration. In the first instance, diaspora engagement policies have to be inclusive so that the marginalized voices of *Dalit* and working-class Punjabis find representation in cultural, academic, and political agendas. The Indian and Punjabi state apparatus must actively collaborate with grassroots diaspora groups that place a high value on equity, education, and social justice. Second, additional investment must be made in rural education, vocational training, and employment generation in Punjab to check distress-induced migration. Drawing from current welfare programmes such as the Pravasi Bharatiya

Bima Yojana, state governments could extend social security initiatives for poor migrants and their families. Third, Partition memory and early migration need to be remembered through inclusive oral history initiatives, archives, and public memorials that capture the diversity of experience by caste, gender, and religion. Finally, psychosocial support systems need to be created for communities continue to be impacted by intergenerational trauma, particularly those displaced or marginalized by Partition and migration's historical forces. Recognizing and addressing these issues through an equitable and historically informed policy framework will not only honour the legacy of early Punjabi migration but also contribute to a more just and inclusive diaspora engagement strategy.

References

Books & Book Chapters

Anderson, B. (1983). *Imagined communities: Reflections on the origin and spread of nationalism.* Verso.

Appadurai, A. (1996). *Modernity at large: Cultural dimensions of globalization.* University of Minnesota Press.

Axel, B.K. (2001). *The nation's tortured body: Violence, representation, and the formation of a Sikh "Diaspora"*. Duke University Press.

Basch, L., Glick Schiller, N., & Szanton Blanc, C. (1994). *Nations unbound: Transnational projects, postcolonial predicaments, and deterritorialized nation-states.* Routledge.

Bhalla, G.S., & Chadha, G.K. (1983). *Green Revolution and the small peasant: A study of income distribution in Punjab agriculture.* Concept Publishing Company.

Bourdieu, P. (1986). "The forms of capital." In J.G. Richardson (Ed.), *Handbook of theory and research for the sociology of education* (pp. 241-258). Greenwood Press.

Butalia, U. (1998). *The other side of silence: Voices from the partition of India.* Duke University Press.

Castles, S. & Miller, M.J. (2009). *The age of migration: International population movements in the modern world* (4th edn.). Palgrave Macmillan.

Dusenbery, V. A. (1995). "A Sikh diaspora? Contested identities and constructed realities." In P. van der Veer (Ed.), *Nation and migration: The politics of space in the South Asian diaspora* (pp. 17-42). University of Pennsylvania Press.

Dusenbery, V.A., & Tatla, D.S. (2009). *Sikh diaspora philanthropy in Punjab: Global giving for local good.* Oxford University Press.

Erikson, E.H. (1968). *Identity: Youth and crisis.* Norton.

Faist, T. (2000). *The volume and dynamics of international migration and transnational social spaces.* Oxford University Press.

Fox, R.G. (1985). *Lions of the Punjab: Culture in the making.* University of California Press.

Giddens, A. (1991). *Modernity and self-identity: Self and society in the late modern age.* Stanford University Press.

Grewal, J.S. (2007). *The Sikhs of the Punjab: Unheard voices of state and guerrilla violence.* Zed Books.

Kaur, R. (2007). *Since 1947: Partition narratives among Punjabi migrants of Delhi.* Oxford University Press.

Levitt, P. (2001). *The transnational villagers.* University of California Press.

Nayyar, D. (1994). *Migration, remittances, and capital flows: The Indian experience.* Oxford University Press.

Portes, A. (1999). "Conclusion: Towards a new world—The origins and effects of transnational activities." *Ethnic and Racial Studies, 22*(2), 463-477.

Putnam, R.D. (2000). *Bowling alone: The collapse and revival of American community.* Simon & Schuster.

Saxenian, A. (2006). *The new Argonauts: Regional advantage in a global economy.* Harvard University Press.

Sen, A. (1999). *Development as freedom.* Oxford University Press.

Sharma, S. (2011). "Punjabi diaspora: Culture, identity, and transnationalism." In A.K. Gera Roy & N. Bhatia (Eds.),

Partitioned lives: Narratives of home, displacement, and resettlement (pp. 123-140). Pearson Education India.

Sassen, S. (1999). *Guests and aliens*. The New Press.

Talbot, I., & Thandi, S. (2004). *People on the move: Punjabi colonial and post-colonial migration*. Oxford University Press.

Tatla, D.S. (1999). *The Sikh diaspora: The search for statehood.* UCL Press.

Vertovec, S. (2009). *Transnationalism*. Routledge.

Wimmer, A., & Glick Schiller, N. (2002). "Methodological nationalism and beyond: Nation-state building, migration, and the social sciences." *Global Networks, 2*(4), 301-334. https://doi.org/10.1111/1471-0374.00043

Journal Articles & Reports

Alam, I., & Ahmed, S. (2018). "India's trade with Gulf Cooperation Council (GCC) countries: A panel gravity model analysis." *ResearchGate*.

Aziz, N., Aziz, A., & Mahar, G. (2023). "Role of provincial migration and immigration in provincial trade of Canada." *Journal of Risk and Financial Management, 16*, 328. https://doi.org/10.3390/jrfm16070328

Berry, J.W. (1997). "Immigration, acculturation, and adaptation." *Applied Psychology: An International Review, 46*(1), 5-34. https://doi.org/10.1111/j.1464-0597.1997.tb01087.x

Chanda, R., & Ghosh, S. (2013). "The Punjabi Diaspora in the UK: An Overview of Characteristics and Contributions to India." *CARIM-India Research Report 2013/25. European University Institute*. https://cadmus.eui.eu/handle/1814/29470

Dhaliwal, S. (2018). "Punjabi International Film Festival: Bridging cultures through cinema." *Journal of Punjab Studies, 25*(2), 45-60.

Farhat, S., & Rather, K.U.I. (2020). "A trade intensity analysis between India and UAE since 2001." *International Journal of Current Engineering and Technology, 10*(2), 1-8. https://doi.org/10.14741/ijcet/v.10.2.1

Gill, A. (2021). "Social entrepreneurship and the Punjabi diaspora: New models of engagement in rural development." *Journal of South Asian Studies, 44*(3), 512-530.

Judge, P.S. (2005). *Punjabis in a transnational context.* Rawat Publications.

Kaur, R. (2020). "Women in the Punjabi diaspora: Negotiating identity, activism, and transnational networks." *Feminist Review, 126*(1), 67-83.

Kumar, S. (2022). "Digital activism and the Punjabi diaspora: The farmers' protest and global solidarity." *International Journal of Media Studies, 29*(2), 289-310.

Kumari, N. (2023). "Fruits of Migration: Seeing Punjabi Diaspora through Its Stories." *The Creative Launcher, 8*(1). https://doi.org/10.53032/tcl.2023.8.1.02

Niumai, A. (2011). "Indian diaspora philanthropy: A sociological perspective." *Man in India, 91*(1), 93-114.

Roy, A.G. (2014). "Imagining Punjab and the Punjabi Diaspora: After More Than a Century of Punjabi Migration." *South Asian Diaspora, 6*(2), 123-130. https://doi.org/10.1080/19438192.2014.934053

Sharma, R. (2015). "Bureaucratic challenges and diaspora engagement in Punjab: An analysis of policy frameworks." *Journal of Migration Studies, 18*(4), 413-435.

Sharma, S. (2020). "Bhangra and beyond: The global rise of Punjabi music." *South Asian Popular Culture, 18*(1), 23-37.

Singh, G. (2016). "The Punjabi diaspora: Global perspectives and challenges." *Diaspora Studies, 9*(1), 50-67.

Singh, G. (2023). "Sikh Separatism and the Brewing Conflict Between Canada and India." *The New Yorker*, September 2023.

Singh, J., & Kaur, P. (2020). "Generational shifts in diaspora engagement: Identity, activism, and digital participation." *Diaspora Studies, 13*(1), 75-93.

Singh, R. (2017). "Contemporary Parvasi (Diasporic) Punjabi Stories: Presentation and Dissemination of Migrant Consciousness." *RESEARCH REVIEW International Journal of Multidisciplinary, 2*(9).

Web Sources & Reports

Government of Punjab. (2021). Punjab economic survey report. Retrieved from https://punjab.gov.in

Punjab Census Report. (2021). Government of Punjab. Retrieved from https://punjab.gov.in

World Bank. (2021). Migration and remittances: Recent developments and outlook. Retrieved from https://www.worldbank.org

Sikh Coalition. (n.d.). Seva and community service. Retrieved from https://www.sikhcoalition.org

International Organization for Migration. (2020). Remittances and sustainable development: Perspectives from developing countries. Retrieved from https://www.iom.int

Index